No Man to Romans

Eocene Epoch to 476 AD

Mary Chris Foxworthy

Cover Art: Dana Bauer

No Man to Romans
Eocene Epoch to 476 AD

First Publish Date 2024
Copyright © 2024 by Equifit

Learn world history in a fun way - through the eyes of a horse!

More books in the Hoofbeats Through History series

Hark! Follow My Hoofbeats - the prequel
Dark to Light - 476 AD - 1250 AD
Armor to Art - 1250 AD - 1600 AD
Muddy Roads to Men on the Moon - 1600 AD - 1961 AD

Be sure to visit the website : www.hoofbeatsthroughhistory.com
The web site provides more information about horses and history.
Hark and his stablemates even have a blog on the site!

Even really smart horses need a little help writing a book so Hark's owner, Mary Chris Foxworthy, helped him. Mary Chris' grandfather owned one of the last creameries in the United States that still used horse-drawn milk wagons. This sparked her life-long love affair with horses and a passion for keeping horse history alive and led to work as a research writer for The Equine Heritage Institute. Mary Chris is also an active exhibitor in Carriage Driving and Dressage.

Acknowledgments

Many thanks to Gloria Austin and the Equine Heritage Institute. Ms. Austin was instrumental in encouraging the creation of the Hoofbeats Through History books. The Equine Heritage Institute provided research information through the library at the Institute.

Art work on pages 9, 17, 29 provided by Patty Urda.

Dear Reader,

Do you love history? I do because I am so much a part of history!

History is the story of who we are, where we come from, and can potentially reveal where we are headed. History is made up of stories that allow us to observe and understand how people and societies behaved.

I am a horse and my name is Hark. Horses have been an important part of human history from the very beginning! The path through history is paved with hoofbeats

If you did not read my first book, "Hark! Follow My Hoofbeats", don't worry, in the first few chapters of this book I will set the stage for you about how horses got on earth in the first place.

I can't wait for you to travel through time with me and learn about amazing events, meet remarkable people and learn about the important contributions horses have made throughout history. I hope you will love history like I do!

Hark

TABLE OF CONTENTS

CHAPTER 1 Only Horses
CHAPTER 2 Horses and the First Humans
CHAPTER 3 Chariots
CHAPTER 4 Rivers and Oceans
CHAPTER 5 They Didn't Know What They Didn't Know
CHAPTER 6 China The Center of the World
CHAPTER 7 What did Ancient Horses Look Like?
CHAPTER 8 When Ancient Egypt Did Not Have Horses
CHAPTER 9 The Israelites Escape Egypt Without Horses
CHAPTER 10 The Assyrians
CHAPTER 11 The Mycenaeans
CHAPTER 12 Homer and the Trojan Horse
CHAPTER 13 Horses and the Ancient Olympics
CHAPTER 14 The Persian Empire and Their Horses
CHAPTER 15 Xenophon and Horsemanship
CHAPTER 16 Alexander the Great and Bucephalus
CHAPTER 17 The Known World is Getting Bigger
CHAPTER 18 Displays of Dominance & Power in Ancient Rome
CHAPTER 19 The Roman Republic
CHAPTER 20 Julius Caesar
CHAPTER 21 Rome, China and Everywhere in Between
CHAPTER 22 The Importance of Rivers – in a New Way!
CHAPTER 23 The Roman Republic Becomes the Roman Empire
CHAPTER 24 Life in the Roman Empire
CHAPTER 25 India
CHAPTER 26 Trade Routes Unite the World – Again
CHAPTER 27 Augustus - The First Roman Emperor
CHAPTER 28 Jesus
CHAPTER 29 What year is it now in this book?
CHAPTER 30 Some Really Bad Emperors and the Praetorian Guard
CHAPTER 31 The Destruction of Jerusalem
CHAPTER 32 Persecution of the Christians and then … Constantine
CHAPTER 33 The Beginning of the End – Goths and Vandals
CHAPTER 34 Here Come the Huns
CHAPTER 35 The Fall of the Roman Empire
SOURCES
INDEX

TIMELINE OF THIS BOOK

Many of the chapters and stories in this book are not written in chronological order. Chronological order refers to the order of events in the time sequence in which they occurred. You can refer to this timeline of the events in the book in order to help you with the chronological order of events, places and people in the book.

Eocene Epoch horses with no humans
5000 BC horses domesticated
3000 BC petroglyphs showing horses
1813 BC – 1644 BC Abraham called by God (approximate birth and death dates of Abraham)
1650 BC Hyksos conquer Egypt and introduce the horse and chariot
1645 BC – 1500 BC Crete destroyed by tidal wave from volcano, Myceneans become first great Greek civilization – first to use horses in battle
1600 BC – 1046 BC Shang Dynasty makes bronze chariot wheels
1570 BC – 1293 BC New Kingdom of Egypt develops a strong army
1500 BC – 500 BC Vedic civilization flourishes in India – foundation of Hinduism
1446 BC Israelites leave Egypt (approximate date)
1400 BC – 1350 BC horses with chariots in tomb paintings in Egypt
1360 BC Mitanni and Hittite horses crossed to produce a superior war horse
1353 BC – 1336 BC Nefertiti and Pharaoh Akhenaten depicted with chariots in tomb paintings
1345 First written information about horses - chariot training manual by Kikkuli
1200 BC – 800 BC Dark Ages of Greece with barbarians in control
1188 BC Trojan War
1100 BC – 771 BC Western Zhou Dynasty extensive use of chariots
1046 BC – 256 BC – China is constantly invaded by nomads of the Steppes on swift horses
1000 BC Nisean horse breed developed (extinct in 1204 AD)
884 BC - 859 BC Assyrians invade Egypt with 4 horse chariots
776 BC – 393 AD Ancient Olympic Games
700 BC First saddle used by Assyrians
600 BC Circus Maximus built in Rome
560 BC Siddhartha Gautama (Buddha) born
539 BC Cyrus the Great conquers Babylon
522 BC – 486 BC Darius the Great is King of Persia
509 BC – 27 BC The Roman Republic
500 BC – 480 BC Persians attempt to conquer Greeks but do not
450 BC First Roman law code written
430 BC Xenophon is born – author of books on training horses

390 BC Rome falls to Celtic invaders

346 BC Alexander the Great acquires Bucephalus

336 BC Phillip of Macedonia is assassinated – his son Alexander takes his throne and begins conquests

326 BC Alexander invades India

323 BC Alexander the Great dies

322 BC Maurya empire in India forms

312 BC Appian Way – first major Roman road is built

300 BC Chinese invent breast strap harness

300 BC Political power of Rome controlled by the Senate

268 BC King Ashoka rules India

264 BC Rome gains control of entire Italian peninsula

221 BC Great Wall of China created by linking walls to prevent invasions from nomads on horses

219 BC Hannibal attacks Saguntum starting the second Punic War and then crosses the Alps

203 BC Hannibal abandons war in Italy and focuses on North Africa

200 BC Chinese develop first solid tree saddle

183 BC Hannibal dies

149 BC – 146 BC Third Punic Wars

138 BC General Zhang Qian goes to Central Asia to make peace with nomads and finds Heavenly Horses

130 BC – 1453 AD Silk Road is major trade route of the known world

102 BC War of the Heavenly Horses

58 BC – 55 BC Julius Caesar conquers Gaul

49 BC – 45 BC Civil War after which Julius Caesar makes himself dictator

44 BC Julius Caesar assassinated

27 BC – 14 AD Augustus is first emperor of Rome

27 BC – 476 AD The Roman Empire

27 BC – 305 AD Praetorian Guard in power

5 BC Jesus Christ is born during the reign of Augustus

14 AD – 37 AD Tiberius is emperor of the Roman Empire

27 AD – 36 AD Jesus preaches

36 AD Jesus is crucified

37 AD - 41 AD Caligula is emperor of the Roman Empire

41 AD – 54 AD Claudius is emperor of the Roman Empire

54 AD – 68 AD Nero is emperor of the Roman Empire

66 AD Jewish revolt

70 AD Fall of Jerusalem and temple burned

70 AD Construction of Coliseum in Rome begins

80 AD Colosseum completed

136 AD Emperor Hadrian exiles the Jewish people

284 AD – 305 AD Diocletian is emperor of the Roman Empire and divides the Empire into Eastern and Western empires

306 AD – 337 AD Reign of Constantine

312 AD Power struggles for control of the Roman Empire - Battle of the Milvian Bridge

312 AD Constantine becomes emperor and moves the Roman capital to the Greek city of Byzantium, which he renames Constantinople

322 AD First evidence of a stirrup on a figurine in China (full collar harness invented by Chinese in 500 AD)

325 AD at the Council of Nicaea Constantine makes Christianity Rome's official religion

370 AD Huns conquer the Alans

395 AD Huns begin to invade Roman lands

402 AD Western Roman Empire moves capital from Rome to Ravenna

402 AD Alaric, King of Visigoths unsuccessfully tries to invade Rome

406 AD Radagaisus, another Visigoth, unsuccessfully tries to invade Rome

406 AD Vandals invade Gaul

410 AD Alaric conquers Rome

422 AD Vandals invade Africa

434 AD Attila becomes King of the Huns

435 AD Rome makes peace treaty with Vandals

439 AD Vandals break peace treaty and advance to Sicily

452 AD Attila ransacks northwestern Italy

455 AD Vandals invade Rome

476 AD Odoacer's forces conquer Rome and he becomes King. The Roman Empire in western Europe, which had been in existence for five hundred years, ceased to exist. A single emperor was replaced by many kings and princes.

CHAPTER 1 ~ Only Horses

Over fifty-five million years ago my ancestors were here on earth. I am a horse and my name is HD Harkness - but you can call me Hark. This is a picture of me in my field. I'm a Morgan horse. My ancestors were here long before there were humans!

Humans have only been here about two hundred thousand years and civilization as we know it is only about six thousand years old.

I am a mammal and I am an herbivore. Over the time of fifty-five million years, there have been a few hundred, now extinct, species of the genus Equus. Today there are only seven species of Equus. My horse family today is quite small. All horse breeds, from slim thoroughbred racehorses to stocky plow horses to tiny ponies, belong to a single species, Equus caballus.

Long before there were breeds of horses like Morgans, horses looked different. The first horses did not look like me at all but over time, horses evolved into a large, four-legged animal that was ultimately domesticated by humans. Learn more about what early horses looked like here: https://www.britannica.com/animal/horse/Evolution-of-the-horse

Horses belong to a group of mammals with an odd number of toes. Mammals with two toes, or "cloven hooves", like goats, pigs, cows, deer and camels do not belong to my family.

My four-toed horse ancestor was very fast. He needed to be fast to evade predators. The middle toe developed into the hoof that I have now; over time it became bigger and better able to provide traction for a fast getaway. The other toes became smaller and eventually disappeared.

Horses now have three "toes" on each leg. Did you know that?! You can see my hoof and if you look closely, you can see the remains of the other two tiny, shrunken toes on the bones above each of my hoofs. These "toes" are called the ergots and the chestnuts.

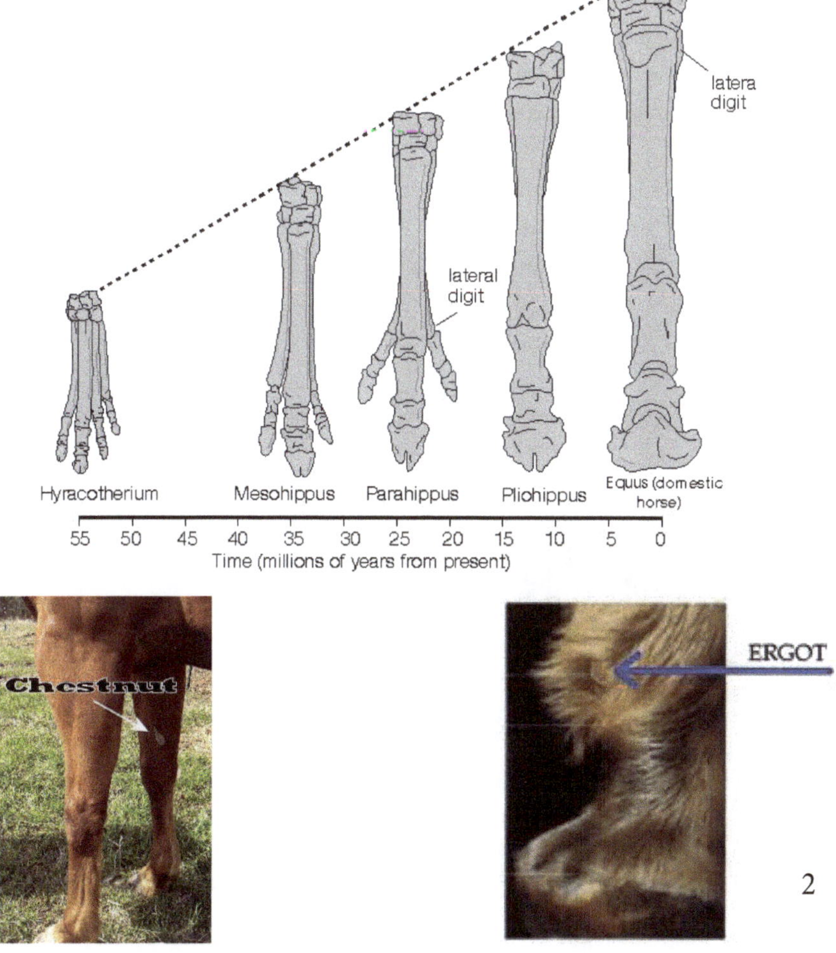

My early relatives ate leaves and fruit but as the world dried out, grasses became available and horse's teeth grew longer, with adaptations for breaking off and crushing the tougher grass. Wide grasslands were perfect for long, swift-legged herbivores and large herds of horses developed.

When humans first saw us, they hunted us and used us for food. Silly humans! It never occurred to them to domesticate us.

Your ancient human ancestors were nomads; they traveled in many directions, constantly in search of abundant food resources and new places to inhabit. But because they traveled on foot, they never traveled very far. They did not know about other civilizations. Imagine a world without a method to communicate other than transporting the message via human runners!

Since there is no written documentation to determine if horses were ridden or driven first, we can only imagine some daring person decided that getting on a horse or hooking a horse to something to pull might be a good idea – and not just to make a video that might go viral!

Using horses for transportation changed the world much like computers and social media have changed the world today. Horses and riders, or horse-drawn carts, could now cover huge distances at great speed. As a result, trade routes developed and cultures began to intermingle. It's hard to imagine, in this age of cars and orbiting space stations, that a horse could be so important to human history – but they are and I can't wait to tell you all about my family!

Prehistoric cave drawings show us that early humans attempted to ride horses.

Horse and rider - Cave painting in Doushe cave, Lorstan, Iran. circa 7-8,000 B.C.

CHAPTER 2 ~ Horses and the First Humans

An archaeologist is a person who studies human history and prehistory by excavating sites and studying the artifacts and physical remains that they find.

Archaeologists have found more than one hundred caves in Europe with paintings of at least four thousand animals. Nearly one third of the animals in painted caves are paintings of my horse ancestors. Almost all of the caves are in southern France and northern Spain. One cave in France, called Chauvet Cave, has been dated to at least thirty-two thousand years ago. Other caves in Lascaux, France and Altamira, Spain are about fifteen thousand years old.

Painting of a horse from a cave in Lascaux France. Learn more about horse cave paintings here: https://www.worldhistory.org/Lascaux_Cave/

Since early humans were nomads that meant that they moved to places where they could find food and water. One of the ways they moved was by following herds of horses. While the horse still remained a "wild animal", humans and horses grew closer together. Humans could attract the horse by providing food and providing shelter. Archaeologists found horse manure in the post holes of what might have been a stable built around 5000 BC in what is now Kazakhstan. Early humans found that they could milk the lactating mares and serve the milk to their own families. Some cultures today still use horses as a source for milk. Knife marks on thousands of ancient horse bones show that horses were raised for meat too.

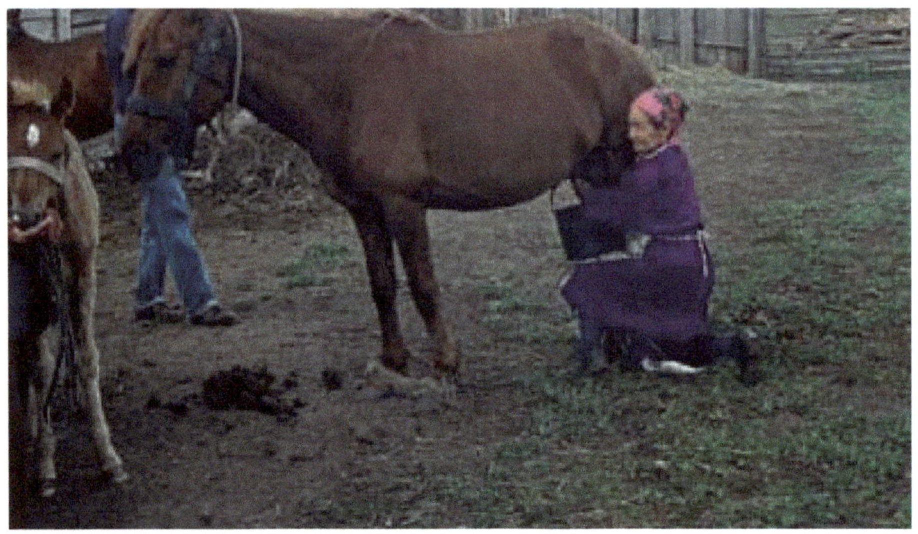

Many cultures still use milk from horses. Learn more about the early domestication of horses in Kazakhstan here: https://www.world-archaeology.com/issues/issue-35/early-date-for-horse-domestication-in-kazakhstan/

The domestication of all animals was a process rather than an event and it occurred slowly over a period of thousands of years in different regions of the world. Cave paintings show us that early humans were very familiar with us; they hunted us, used us for milk and eventually did ride us. Most of these developments occurred before writing was invented so we depend on archaeological evidence to help us understand what happened.

I am so glad that humans figured out how to partner with the horse because the domestication of my ancestors represents one of the most important turning points in human history! Archaeological evidence tells us that horses were domesticated about 5000 BC.

The first known written information about horses was in 1345 BC. In 1345 BC a Mitannian horse-master known as Kikkuli wrote the "Chariot Training Manual". It gave a detailed plan for training and caring for horses. Wow! Chariots! Why would my ancestors need to pull a chariot?

Kikkuli text. Clay tablet, a training program for chariot horses. 14th century BC. Vorderasiatisches Museum, Berlin. Learn more about the Kikkuli text here: http://worksofchivalry.com/ kikkuli/

Remember, most people at the time were nomads who moved from place to place to find food and water so it was important to have control of valuable hunting lands and places with water. When the chariot was invented, those who first used the new invention were able to storm their neighbors and seize valuable hunting and pasturing land rights.

The chariot became the supreme military weapon. Chariots were light vehicles on two wheels, pulled by one or more horses. Usually there were two people in a chariot and they were both standing. One person was the driver and the other one was the fighter; he would have a bow and arrow or a javelin.

The oldest evidence of chariots to date comes from petroglyphs found in Armenia from 3000 BC. Petroglyphs are ancient rock carvings. The petroglyphs found in Armenia are the oldest pictures of men driving chariots.

An ancient burial containing chariots and gold artifacts was discovered by archaeologists in the country of Georgia. The burial site, which would've been intended for a chief, dates back over 4,000 years to a time archaeologists call the Early Bronze Age. Learn more about this discovery here: https://www.livescience.com/46491-early-bronze-age-chariot-burial-photos.html

This bronze model of a chariot was found by archaeologists in one of the tombs in Lchashen in Armenia and is thought to be from the Bronze Age which was 3000 BC – 1200 BC.

When Kikkuli wrote the "Chariot Training Manual" he knew that if he could find a way to train horses to be fast and strong then the kingdom of Matanni, where he lived, would have an advantage over the people who wanted to invade them.

The Kingdom of Mitanni spread from northern Mesopotamia down through Anatolia (which is modern-day Iraq through Turkey). You've probably heard of Egypt. The Kingdom of Mitanni was important enough at that time to have alliances with mighty Egypt. They both needed to protect themselves from the threat of Hittite domination, they needed to defend themselves from many attacks and invasions.

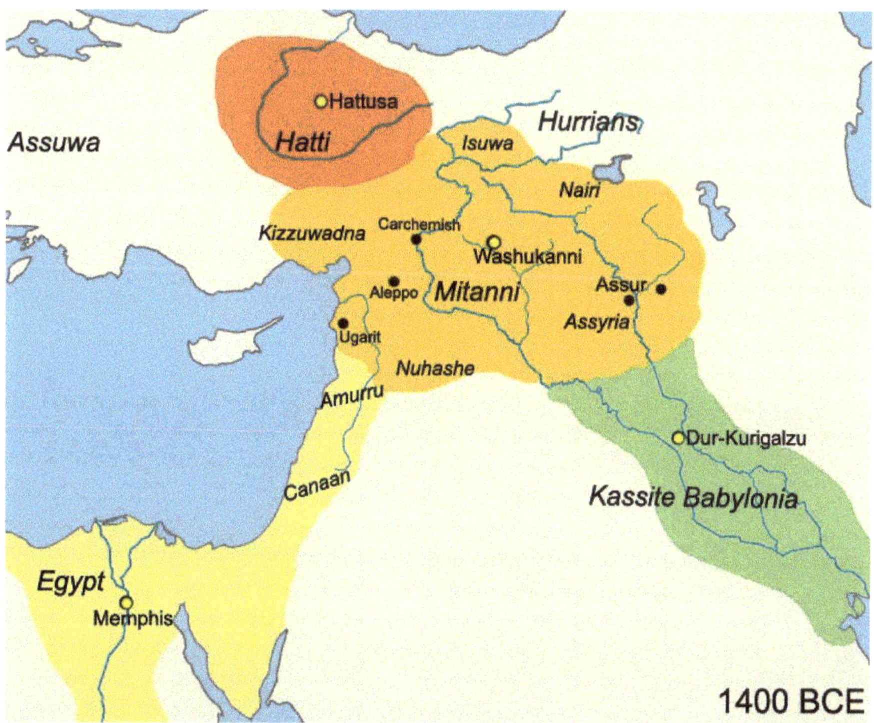

Kikkuli knew that a well-trained, athletic horse was needed to pull the chariots. He developed a new method of training called "interval train-ing". My ancestors were very happy to be trained in a way that made them healthy and fit for what they had to do. One of my ancient relatives, a horse named Thebes, was trained by Kikkuli. He would like to tell you about his training.

My human trainer has great plans for me.

I am Thebes, a horse in the stables in the Kingdom of
Mitanni. My trainer knows that a well-trained, athletic horse
is what is needed to rival the mighty power of those who want
to attack and invade our land.

My trainer, Kikkuli, has developed a new method of training
called "interval training". I often pace a league – that's about
three and a half miles – then I run a furlong – that's about two
hundred twenty yards. That exercise is followed by rest and
then more exercise. Every few days I am asked to do more
than the day before and my rest and feed are increased as
needed.

There are always many baths included too. My care is the
best so that I will become a mighty horse in the stables
Mitanni!

Interval training is still used today to strengthen the horse's muscles and respiratory system - just like in the days of Kikkuli in 1345 BC. Even human athletes do interval training. What a smart man Kikkuli was to develop this system of training!

Eventually, everywhere in Europe, the Middle East, India and China, kings, great pharaohs and even lesser known rulers used the chariot as their master weapon. Ancient art work created to honor the rulers shows them riding in chariots. They even included chariots and horses in their tombs as symbols of power. Chariots were also used for hunting purposes and in sporting contests such as the Ancient Olympic Games and in the Roman Circus Maximus. We'll learn more about that later – it's exciting!

Unlike technology today, that becomes out of date very rapidly, the use of the chariot declined very slowly starting around 500 BC. People still lived far apart and did not have a way to communicate and share information so some parts of Europe were just learning about chariots while other parts of the world had already been using chariots for hundreds of years!

The horse came to be a valuable military asset - no longer just a food source of the nomads. Horse breeding became very important. Kingdoms and powerful rulers aspired to have large stables to supply their armies with horses for their chariots.

In ancient times there were no roads. People built cities near rivers so that they could have water to drink and water for their crops. Cities also grew up near rivers because it was easier to ship goods up and down the river than to try and transport it across land. In ancient times wheels were made out of wood and carts with large loads were too difficult to pull on

the wooden wheels across the sandy and rocky and sometimes mountain-ous land. People had not figured out a way to use horses yet to help them transport things and horses in ancient times were much smaller than they are now so, they were not as strong.

Bronze Age (3300BC - 1200 BC) wooden wheel.

Since people only traveled by rivers it limited where they could go. They did not meet people from other lands that did not live near the river that flowed near their city and they did not learn about all the discoveries and inventions made by other people.

People in China, people in India, people in Egypt and people in Europe all lived near rivers but they did not know much about each other. Each culture was discovering things not knowing what the other one was doing or discovering.

But one thing all peoples were doing almost everywhere was figuring out how to partner with my horse ancestors.

While the people in Egypt, Armenia, Babylon, Hatti and Matanni were using chariots to invade each other, the Chinese and other people were learning how to partner with the horse in many more ways.

Are you wondering if there were horses in the Americas at this time?
Fifty-five million years ago the dinosaurs were gone and mammals roamed
the earth.

Through the study of fossils, paleontologists have found that my horse
ancestors originated, lived and evolved in North America and eventually
migrated around the globe. The planet looked much different then. Millions of years ago my horse ancestors were able to travel to Eurasia by
crossing the Bering land bridge.

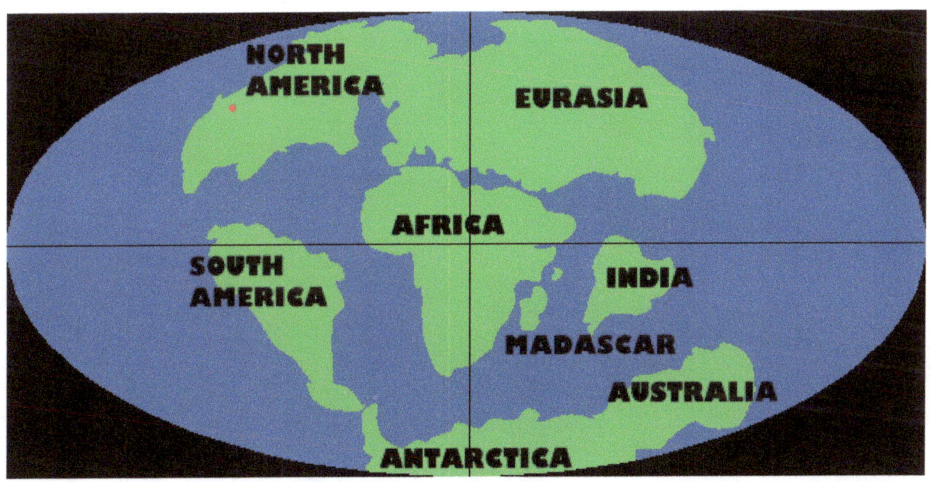

How the world looked millions of years ago

Eventually horses disappeared in the Americas. There were no horses at all
in the Americas for thousands and thousands of years! Why? Where did all
of the horses go?

12

Slowly the Earth began to change. In North America the mountain ranges began to uplift. In the center of the continents the climate became dryer. Lakes dried; their once-muddy bottoms eventually formed rock. The forests gave way to grassy plains. Seasons became more evident and ice began to form at the poles.

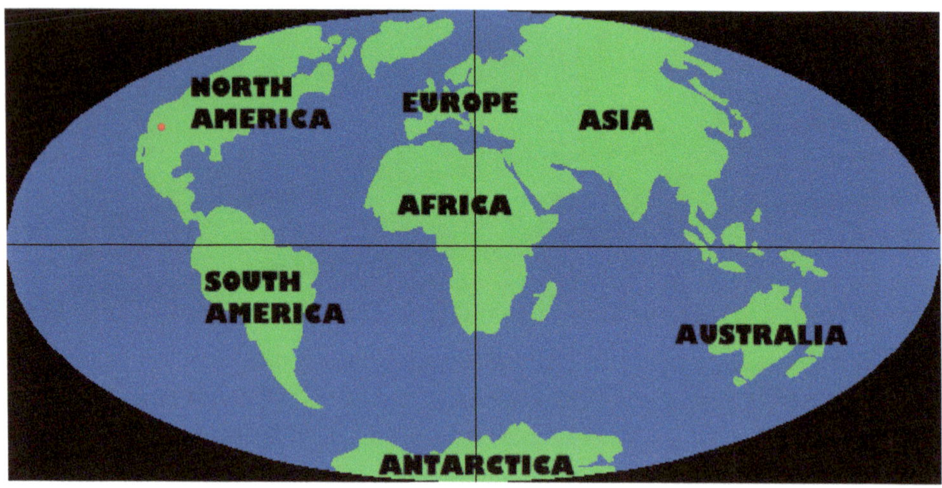

The continents broke and drifted apart and the horses could not get back to the Americas Can you see how this picture looks different than the one on the previous page?

Even though my horse ancestors lived in the Americas in prehistoric times, the horse, as we know it today, did not come back to the Americas until the 1500's when the Spanish, French and English started to explore the New World. I'll tell you all about that in another book.

Can you imagine not knowing anything about other places in the world? In ancient times they did not have the Internet and telephones and radios. They did not even have newspapers. Today, technology changes almost monthly and when cures for illnesses and diseases are discovered, the information can be shared instantly. In ancient times, there was no way for people to know about other parts of the world unless someone traveled there and came back and told people about it. In some places in the world people were not even riding or driving horses yet so travel was on foot only! We already learned that some parts of Europe were just learning about chariots while other parts of the world had already been using chariots for hundreds of years. In the ancient world, there was no way for people of one area to know how people lived in another area. They didn't know what other people looked like and most likely, they even spoke a different language. They had no way of knowing about the discoveries and inventions made by people in distant lands.

Long ago, the Sahara Desert in Africa was a lush, fertile grassland with many animals and people. As the climate changed, the area turned into the desert that it is today. Do you wonder how the climate changed so long ago when there were no cars, pollution and millions of people? 22,000 to 10,500 years ago the Sahara was devoid of any human occupation outside the Nile Valley and extended 250 miles further south than it does today. 10,500 to 9,000 years ago monsoon rains begin sweeping into the Sahara, transforming the region into a habitable area swiftly settled by Nile Valley dwellers. 9,000 to 7,300 years ago continued rains, vegetation growth and animal migrations lead to well established human settlements, including the introduction of domesticated livestock such as sheep and goats. 7,300 to 5,500 years ago the monsoonal rains stopped and the area became very dry, prompting humans to move to other habitable areas.

For centuries the people in southern Africa were cut off from the rest of the world by the vast desert. The people in southern Africa region did not leave mummies and tombs and clay tablets so we knew very little about this area of Africa until the medieval era, thousands of years later!

The horse has been very important throughout the history of the "Middle Kingdom". Did you know that China is sometimes called the "Middle Kingdom"?

Why did China call itself the "Middle Kingdom"? Throughout the last five thousand years, China has been known by many different names but the most traditional name that China has used to refer to itself is Zhonggou which means "Middle Kingdom". The people in China believed that their country was the "center" of the world in a cultural and historical way so that is why they called themselves the "Middle Kingdom". Did you know that the Chinese invented the stirrup, and the horse collar as well as an effective way to harness horses to carts and wagons?

During the Western Zhou Dynasty (1100 BC - 771 BC) military strength was measured by the number of war chariots each kingdom had. Horses were so important to the Chinese that horses, and the vehicles they pulled, were buried with their owners for the afterlife.

Shang Dynasty (1660 BC - 1046 BC) buried chariots

A dynasty means that one family keeps control of the country for many, many years - passing the crown along from father to son. Many dynasties in China lasted hundreds of years.

Archaeologists discovered the first use of bronze was in Serbia in 4500 BC. During the Shang Dynasty in China, which lasted from 1600 BC to 1046 BC (wow that's 554 years) the Chinese started using bronze. They made weapons, wheels and farming tools out of bronze. Most of the people in ancient China were farmers. They grew a type of grain that the people in Mesopotamia and Egypt could not grow; they grew rice. Rice will only grow in a place where the ground is very wet most of the year.

In the fourth century BC, during the Eastern Zhou Dynasty which lasted from 770 BC to 221 BC (549 years!), the Chinese invented a harness with a breast strap known as the "trace harness" (b) in the third century BC they developed the collar (c.) Before this time horses were hooked to carts using a throat-and-girth harness (a) which choked a horse and made it very hard for the horse to pull efficiently. The collar harness allowed a single horse to haul a ton and a half. The people in Europe did not know about the trace harness until the sixth century AD – that's one thousand years!

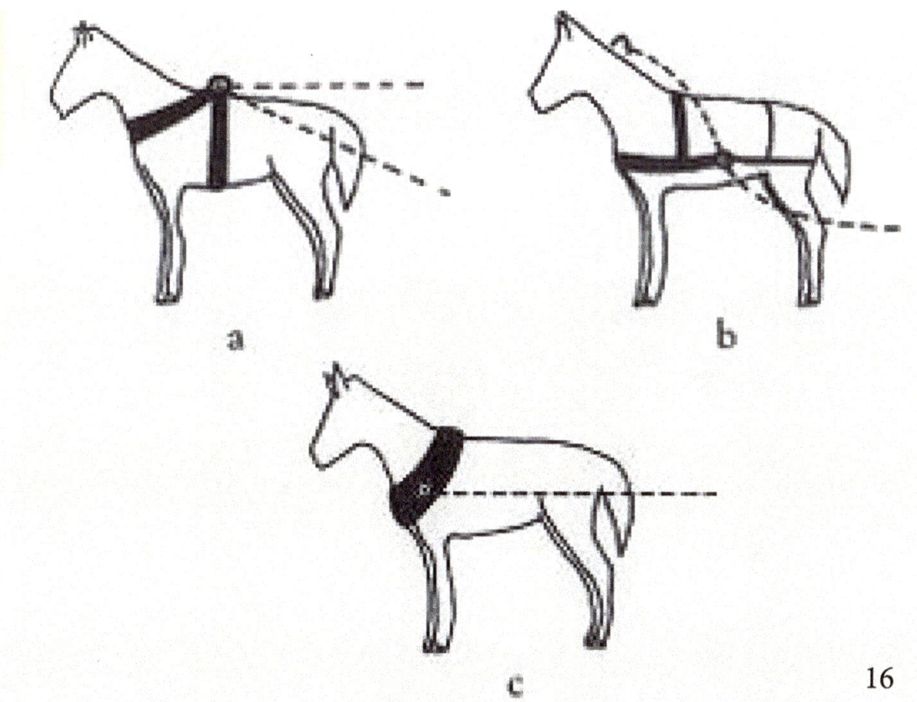

The earliest known evidence of a modern-style stirrup was also found in China on a ceramic horse figurine that was buried in a First Jin Dynasty Chinese tomb near Nanjing in 322 AD. Stirrups did not appear in the West until 400 years later.

The stirrup is an invention that changed the history of the world. Stirrups are simple devices made of a pair of frames or rings attached to the saddle of a horse with straps. Why do you think the stirrup would be so important? One of my distant relatives from ancient China would like to tell you about that.

My name is Liang, I am a horse living in ancient China. Can you even imagine how a person would get on me without stirrups? A rider would have to do a flying leap to get on me and sometimes, when they landed, it hurt my back. Other horses are not as kind as I am and disliked it so much that they would run off and try to get rid of their rider when they jumped on. Once on me, the rider had to grip tightly with their thighs or hold on to my mane to avoid falling off. A rider supported by stirrups was less likely to fall off while fighting and could deliver a blow with a weapon that was able to take advantage of my weight and momentum! The stirrup has been described as one of the most important inventions in the history of warfare. I would have to agree!

The first saddle-like equipment was used by the Assyrians in about 700 BC. These were fringed cloths or pads that were held on with a girth or surcingle around the horse's middle and included straps around the horse's chest and cruppers; (cruppers are straps that go down the horses back and under the tail.) That's a lot of straps to hold something on! The Chinese were the first to develop a solid treed saddle during the Han Dynasty in about 200 BC. These saddles were made of felt that covered a wooden frame. This type of saddle kept a rider's weight off the horse's back and improved the health of the horse and lengthened the time he was able to work.

solid tree saddle 200BC

The Chinese are credited with many ancient discoveries and inventions. According to Chinese legend, tea was first discovered by Shennong, Chinese Father of Agriculture, around 2737 BC.

18

Silk, one of the oldest fibers, originated in China as early as six thousand years ago. Chinese people mastered silk weaving and closely guarded the secret to making silk. The West had to pay gold of the same weight for the silk. In ancient times the silk was a very important item made in China and for many centuries merchants transported this precious item from China to the West, forming the famous "Silk Road". We'll learn more about the Silk Road later.

"The Yellow Emperor's Classic of Medicine" is an ancient book on health and disease. It is said to have been written by the famous Chinese emperor Huangdi around 2600 BC but some people think he is a mythical person and the book probably dates from around 300 BC. The book is written as a discussion between Huangdi and his physician. In the book Huangdi asks his physician about how to stay healthy, avoid disease and what treatments can be used for illnesses and pain. The book is an important source about traditional Chinese medicine even today.

From my point of view, as a horse, I think it makes sense that the Chinese thought of their country as the "Center of the World". After all, the Chinese invented many things and especially things that really helped horses to work together with humans. Despite the Chinese developing so many things for horses, the Chinese army did not have enough good quality horses because the climate was not good and there was not enough fodder (fodder is the dried hay that horses eat). Their neighbors, the people of the Steppe region, had wonderful horses. The Steppe region of northern central Eurasia was known in ancient times for its horse breeding and horse-riding nomad peoples. The nomads of the Steppe regions had many well-bred horses. These nomadic barbarians were excellent horsemen and archers. On their agile horses they could move in swiftly and make attacks on China.

The vast Eurasian Steppe was a fertile ground for breeding horses.

19

The Chinese were indeed more cultured but they were at a disadvantage when it came to protecting themselves.

Ancient China and the Steppes

The horse had such an important influence on the Middle Kingdom that some historians think that the Great Wall was built against the horse, since the country lived under the constant threat of invasion from the nomads of the Steppe region with their swift horses. During the Western Zhou Dynasty (1046 BC – 771 BC) and the Eastern Zhou Dynasty Period (770 BC – 256 BC) several powerful states were established in China. In order to defend themselves, they all built walls and stationed troops on their borders. In 221 BC, Emperor Qin Shi Huang unified China for the first time after defeating the other states. Since China was constantly under attack by the barbarians from the Steppes, he ordered that the sections of the Great Wall, created by different states, be linked together and extended. Over the following 2,500 years, more than twenty states and dynasties played a part in building the Great Wall. The length of the wall exceeds thirteen thousand one hundred seventy miles!

20

The Great Wall protected the provinces of ancient China, which lay to the south of the Great Wall, from the threat from the Steppes which were to the north of the Great Wall.

CHAPTER 7 ~ What did Ancient Horses Look Like?

Have you been wondering about what types of horses they had in ancient times and what they looked like?

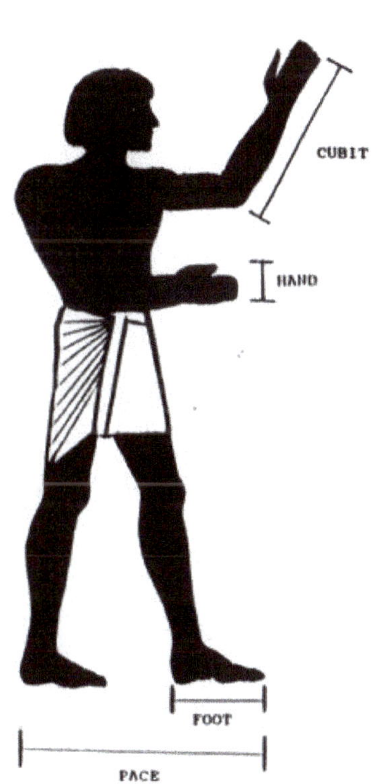

Horses in ancient times were much smaller than they are now. Most horses were only about 12 to13 hands high. The average horse now is 15 to 16 hands high. Horses were, and still are, measured by how many hands high they are from the ground to the withers. One of the oldest units of length measurement used in the ancient world was the 'cubit' which was the length of the arm from the tip of the finger to the elbow. This could then be subdivided into shorter units like the foot, hand (which at 4 inches is still used today for expressing the height of horses) or some units were added together to make longer units like the pace.

But just think, everyone's hands and forearms and feet are different sizes so in ancient times it was usually the king's dimensions which were used as the norm.

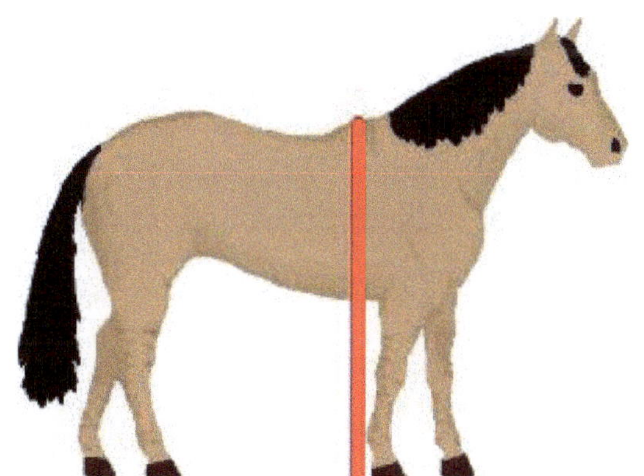

We've already learned that the Hittites were very powerful and attacked many of the regions surrounding their sprawling kingdom. They brought horses with them wherever they went and introduced the horse to many cultures. Their horses rank among the first horses in the Middle East.

In 1500 BC the Mittani people allied with Egypt to protect themselves from the Hittites. One of the most mysterious and powerful women in ancient Egypt was Nefertiti. Nefertiti was queen alongside Pharaoh Akhenaten from 1353 to 1336 BC. On the walls of tombs and temples built during Akhenaten's reign Nefertiti is shown alongside her husband more often than any other Egyptian queen. In many paintings she is shown in positions of power and authority driving a chariot.

In this tomb painting in the tomb of Meryre, high priest of the Aten, Queen Nefertiti is shown smaller and follows the Pharaoh. Like him, she drives her chariot, drawn by a team of horses, whip in hand and without a driver. The famous horses of Nefertiti were probably Mittani.

Even though we can't see the entire painting, archaeologists have been able to determine what the original painting may have looked like.

In the colored wall painting, Nefertiti's horses look like they may have been chestnuts (bright orange colored). Ancient horses seem to be many colors. In the private tomb of Menna, which was constructed from 1400 BC to 1390 BC, there are even spotted horses!

Nebamun was the accountant in charge of grain at the great Temple of Amun at Karnak around 1350 BC. This scene from his tomb-chapel shows officials inspecting fields with white and black horses.

Do you think that some of these tomb paintings of ancient horses look like me?

In 1360 BC, after the death of Tushratta, the last king of the Mittani, a war resulted and Mittani became part of the Hittite Empire. Mittani and Hittite horses were crossed to produce a superior horse suitable for war, chariot pulling, and racing. This is when Kikkuli wrote the "Chariot Training Manual".

In 1000 BC, a new breed of horse was being developed in Central Asia. The name of the breed was Nisean and it is now extinct. The Nisean, was tall and swift and came in many colors; they were dark bay, white, chestnut and seal brown, but also rarer colors such as black, roan, palomino, and various spotted patterns. The Nisean was the mount of the nobility in ancient Persia. The ancient Greeks called the horse "Nisean" after the town Nisa where the horse was bred. Nisa was in Media which is now Turkmenistan. The Chinese called the horse the Tien Ma - the Heavenly Horse. The Nisean horse was the most valuable horse in the ancient world.

The Nisean horse was very important for a very long time. They did not become extinct until the conquest of Constantinople in 1204 AD! Many Iberian type horses today are thought to be related to the Nisean. The Iberian Peninsula of southwest Europe contains the countries of Spain, Portugal, Andorra, and Gibraltar as well as a very small portion of France. Today there are seventeen breeds of horses that are from the Iberian Peninsula. Do you think I might be related to the Nisean horse?

26

We've learned about chariots in Egypt and you have seen pictures from tombs of horses in Egypt. Did you know though that the ancient Egyptians learned about horses and chariots from another culture that had horses and chariots long before the Egyptians had them?

By 1782 BC, Egypt had developed as a civilization for over two thousand years. The possibility of a people invading their country and gaining control would have seemed as silly to them as a full-scale invasion of earth by flying saucers from Mars would be by us today.

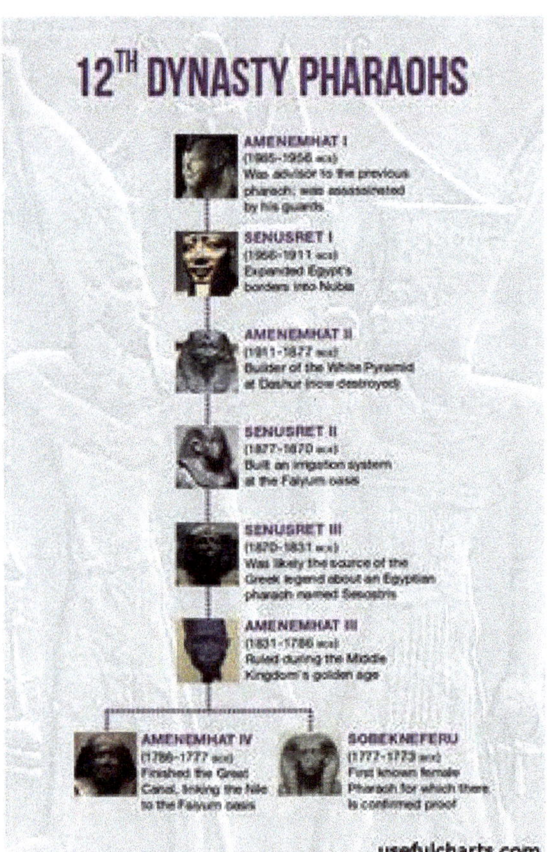

The Twelfth Dynasty (1991 BC – 1786 BC) was the high point of Egyptian culture and is called the "classical age" of Egypt. The Thirteenth Dynasty (1786 BC – 1633 BC) was not as strong and made many bad decisions. One bad decision was to move the capital to Thebes in Upper Egypt. This left Lower Egypt open and allowed many different people to move in and gain control. Through commerce, port towns quickly grew and attracted many of the people known to the Egyptians as "Asiatics".

The Hyksos, a people of mixed Semitic and Asiatic descent, gained control of the area and then moved north making treaties with various rulers of regions in Lower Egypt until they had taken a large amount of the land and were able to gain power. The innovations of the Hyksos transformed the culture of Egypt. Trade flourished during the time of the Hyksos. The Hyksos ruled for a long time.

27

Ahmose I overthrew the Hyksos and founded the Eighteenth Dynasty (1570 BC – 1293 BC). This initiated the period of the New Kingdom of Egypt, the era of the Egyptian empire. He developed a professional Egyptian army of conquest to make sure that no foreign people like the Hyksos would ever be able to gain such power in the land of Egypt ever again.

Egyptian art from the New Kingdom shows the pharaoh kings, such as Tutankhamun and Ramesses II, in their chariots hunting with their dogs and going to war. The New Kingdom is the period most familiar to people in the present day so that is why the chariot is associated with Egypt. The Egyptians had no knowledge of the chariot or the horses that pulled chariots however, until it was introduced by the Hyksos.

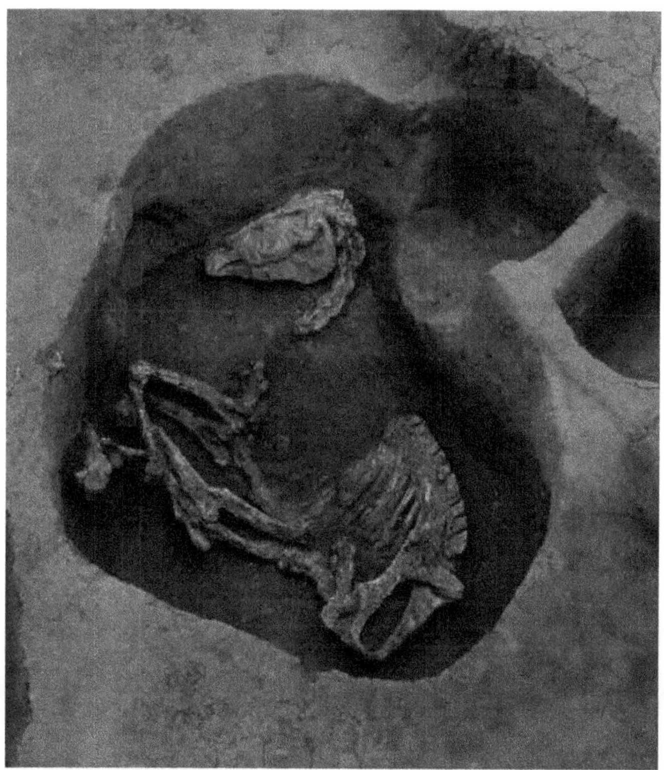

The earliest horse burial in Egypt was excavated at Avaris, the capital of Egypt under the Hyksos. This is evidence of the many innovations, including the horse and chariot, that the Hyksos brought with them that would have a lasting impact on the course of Egyptian history.

The Hyksos also introduced the Egyptians to the compound bow, the short sword and the bronze dagger. New methods of crop irrigation were introduced by the Hyksos as well as new fruit and vegetable cultivation practices. They also introduced an improved potter's wheel that resulted in higher quality ceramics that were also more durable and they brought to Egypt the vertical loom, which produced better quality linen.

Egypt was able to achieve its largest empire and greatest power by the addition of the horse and chariot that were first introduced to the Egyptians by the Hyksos. When the Hyksos were expelled, all traces of the Hyksos in Egypt were erased until archaeologists were able to discover their existence so, no wonder everyone thinks the Egyptians had chariots and horses for a much longer time than they really did. Can you see why it is so important to understand and learn from the past and not erase history ?

CHAPTER 9 ~ The Israelites Escape Egypt Without Horses

Abraham was a man living in Ur and like most people at the time he believed there were many gods. One day he heard a voice from heaven telling him that there was only one true God. God told Abraham to move with his family to Canaan. This new nation of people started by Abraham was called the Israelites.

Abraham had a son named Isaac and Isaac had a son named Jacob. Jacob had twelve sons! One of those was a boy named Joseph. Jacob loved Joseph very much and that made his brothers jealous so they sold Joseph into slavery to travelers from Egypt. Once in Egypt, the pharaoh discovered that Joseph could interpret dreams. Joseph was able to interpret many dreams that kept the land of Egypt safe and happy so the pharaoh gave Joseph a position of importance. Back in Canaan there was a famine and the Israelites were starving. They heard that there was plenty of food and water in Egypt so they left for Egypt. Joseph had pity on them and convinced the pharaoh to allow them to stay.

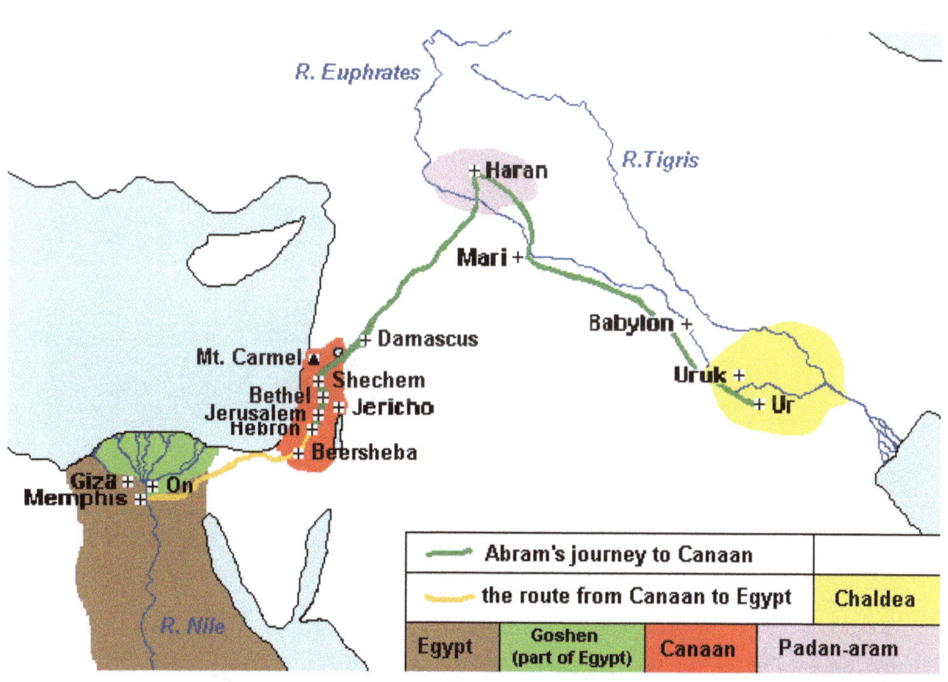

The Israelite nation began to grow and prosper in Egypt. This scared the Egyptians. They thought, "What if they take over like the Hyksos did?" So, the Egyptians made the Israelites their slaves.

The Pharaoh became so worried that he told his soldiers to kill all the new babies born of the Israelites. One very frightened mother put her baby in a basket in the river. The Pharaoh's daughter found the baby and named him Moses. The baby's mother became his nurse in the palace of the pharaoh.

When Moses grew up, he told the pharaoh that he was an Israelite and he did not like that the pharaoh was treating the Israelites so badly. He asked the pharaoh to "let my people go." The pharaoh did not want to lose all of his slaves so he would not do that. God sent many plagues upon the Egyptians and finally the pharaoh let the Israelites go free. But he did not really mean that so, he sent his soldiers after them. When the Israelites got to the Red Sea the water parted and they walked through. When the Egyptians got there with their horses and chariots, the sea closed in on them and the Israelites were able to escape from Egypt.

For many years the Israelites looked for a new home. This was called the Exodus. When the Israelites finally arrived in Canaan to settle, they were not the only people there. The Phoenicians were already living in Canaan. The land in Canaan was not good for raising grains or livestock but it was close to the Mediterranean Sea. The Phoenicians became great sailors and made boats to travel out to sea and settle other areas. One of the famous cites they settled was Carthage around 814 BC.

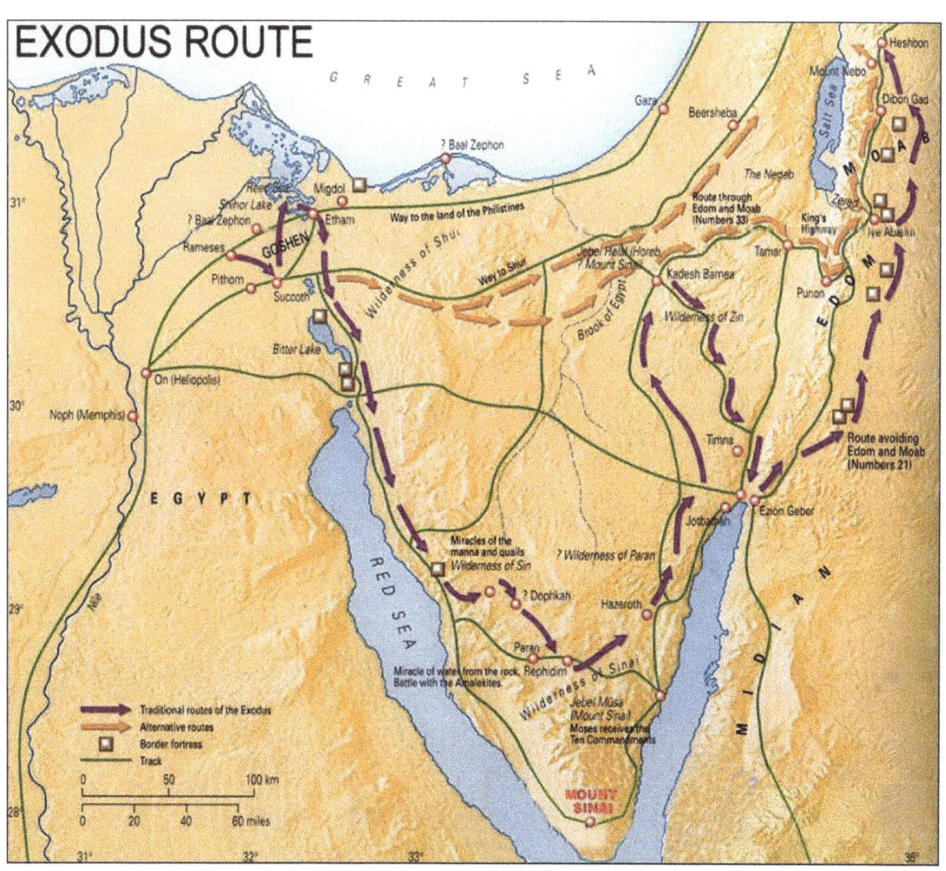

Are you wondering why, when the Israelites escaped from Egypt, the only horses at the Red Sea were the drowned Egyptian horses? The Israelites did not have any horses to help them with their escape. They had no pack horses to carry their supplies or for them to ride during their Exodus. It wasn't because they were so primitive that they hadn't invented wheels for chariots. They probably built chariots for the pharaoh when they were slaves in Egypt. In most of the battles in the Bible the Israelites do not have a cavalry or chariots.

In Deuteronomy, one of the books of the Bible, it says that "Moreover, he shall not multiply horses for himself, nor shall he cause the people to return to Egypt to multiply horses, since the Lord has said to you, You shall never again return that way." Horses were needed for war to pull the chariots. Multiplying horses was showing a warlike spirit and meant that the people had more faith in making a great army to protect them than having faith in God to protect them. Horses were also a way to escape the battle. When an army was on foot there could be no retreat and many Israelites believed that Israel must believe in God for the promised victory. If Israel was walking with God, victory was assured. No need to flee. They believed that they had God's promise. Many Israelites believed that the times their leaders disobeyed God and used horses is when they were defeated.

CHAPTER 10 ~ The Assyrians

Assyria is an area located in Upper Mesopotamia, and named after the
Assyrians. Most of their cities were located along the Tigris River.

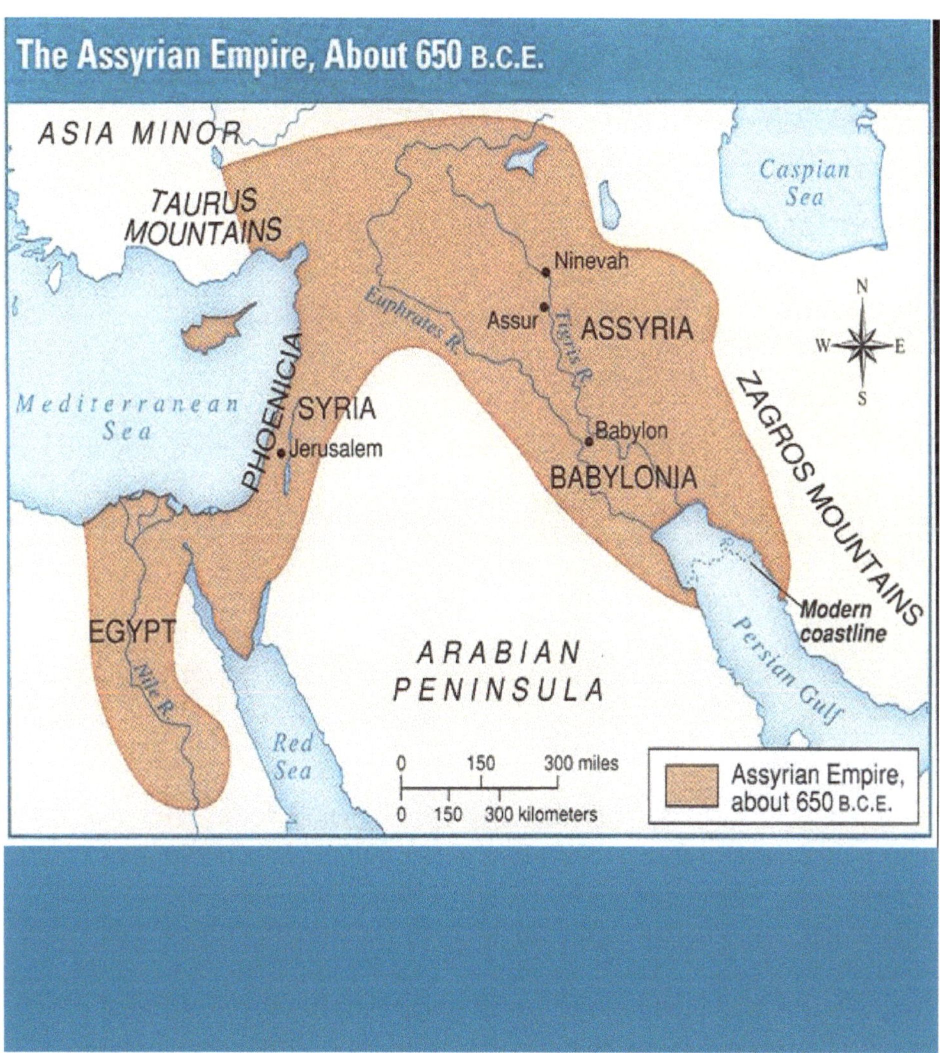

Assyrians became an aggressive people under the rule of King Ashurnasirpal II who reigned from 884 to 859 BC. He invaded the lands of his
neighbors up and down the Tigris and Euphrates Rivers. His army invaded Canaan and forced the Israelites out of Canaan. They marched into
Asia Minor and forced the people there to obey them too. Then they even
marched into mighty Egypt and took that over too.   34

Why were the Assyrians able to conquer so many countries and kingdoms? Partly because they were the first to organize their army into units with commanders and…mostly because…they had horse power! They built large powerful chariots that could be pulled by four horses. Can you imagine that? That would be much more powerful than the chariots owned by other armies. They also built roads large enough for their wheeled vehicles to move their armies and equipment quickly to where they were needed. They built battering rams to knock down walls and ladders to climb walls too. They were very brutal and cruel which allowed them to easily conquer territories.

This marble slab is from Ashurnasirpal II's palace. It is now in the British Museum. The image shows Ashurnasirpal II and his army advancing against a town. A battering ram is being drawn on a six-wheeled carriage.

Nineveh was the capital of the Assyrian empire. It was one of the most beautiful cities in the world at the time with its gardens, temples and splendid palaces. Nineveh had carefully planned canals and aqueducts to make sure that a steady supply of water was available not only for human consumption but also to keep the public parks and gardens irrigated. The kings who ruled Nineveh believed that the glory of Nineveh would last forever. Eventually though, the Babylonians were able to conquer the Assyrians.

CHAPTER ~ 11 The Mycenaeans

Many of the people we have learned about so far lived on land near rivers. There were people in other parts of the world who lived in areas surrounded by water. You might think that horses were not important to these people then but they were.

The Minoans lived on the island of Crete in the Mediterranean Sea. Crete had been inhabited since 7000 B.C. The culture that developed there spread throughout the entire eastern Mediterranean world. Crete's command of the seas allowed its stunning art and architecture to deeply influence the Greek civilization that would succeed it.

A volcano followed by a tidal wave devastated the island of Crete sometime between 1645 BC and 1500 BC. The once prosperous Minoans were now just a ragged people. Historians believe this one event changed the history of the ancient world

Eventually the island recovered and people from the city of Mycenae, in Greece, took over the island.

Mycenae was not the only big city in Greece at the time. Athens and Thebes were also big and important cites but the Mycenaeans had something those cites did not have – they were the first people from Greece to use horses in battle. With their weapons and large chariots pulled by horses, they were able to take over the entire region of the Aegean Sea. They were the first great Greek civilization.

This picture from a gravestone in Mycenae is from 1500 BC and is thought to be one of the oldest pictures of a chariot from that area.

The Mycenaeans were surrounded by barbarians. Barbarians did not come from any one country. They were called barbarians because they were primitive and not civilized but they were very strong and brutal. Eventually the barbarians were able to conquer the entire area. But because they could not read or write, and they spent most of their time burning cites, we don't know much about them. This was called the Dark Ages of Greece from 1200 BC to 800 BC.

37

CHAPTER 12 ~ Homer and the Trojan Horse

Eventually the people who settled in Greece became civilized and developed an alphabet and a way to write and tell stories. Homer was a man who lived in Greece around 700 BC but some people think he may have lived in 1200 BC. Homer lived before a dating system was in place so it is difficult to give someone a birth date when he was born before there was a calendar. Homer wrote a poem called "The Iliad" and then he wrote another story called "The Odyssey". Both of these stories told the story of the Trojan War.

Trojans are the people who lived in Troy. The Trojan War began when the Trojan prince, Paris, captured Queen Helen of Sparta. Helen's husband, Menelaus, convinced his brother Agamemnon, king of Mycenae, to lead an expedition to rescue her. Agamemnon was joined by the Greek heroes Achilles, Odysseus, Nestor and Ajax. They traveled in a fleet of more than a thousand ships. They crossed the Aegean Sea to Asia Minor to lay siege to Troy and demand Helen's return.

Hector leaving for the Trojan war

Troy was famous for its horse breeding. Homer refers to Troy as a place where horses are bred and tamed. Hector was Troy's greatest warrior and Homer called him "tamer of horses". In his stories Homer tells how much Hector loved horses and that he was a good husband and father.

The war lasted ten years until the Greeks decided to outwit Troy. Many Greek soldiers pretended to set sail for home, acting as if they had given up. In the midst of this pretend evacuation they made a large wooden horse and left it, as a supposed gift, at the gates of Troy. Troy loved horses so this seemed like an honorable gift!

The Trojans pulled the mysterious gift into the city. When night fell, the horse opened up and a group of Greek warriors climbed out and opened the gates of the city to let the Greek army enter the city and conquer Troy.

Would a Trojan horse work today? Have you heard of Trojan viruses on your computer? They are called Trojans because they look like something you should open but when you do, bad things happen to your computer.

You have read about how my ancient horse relatives were important in battle and transportation. In ancient times, horses were also very important in sports.

The Ancient Olympic Games took place every four years in Olympia in Greece from 776 BC to at least 393 AD. The Ancient Olympics were so important that when the Persians invaded Greece in the summer of 480 BC, Greece had a very hard time getting an army together because so many people wanted to go to the Olympics. So, they actually had to delay putting the army together to defend their own country from invaders.

Chariot Racing was a sport in the Ancient Olympics. Chariot Racing is one of the most thrilling and danger-filled sports ever invented by man. The four-horse chariot race was the most popular, prestigious and long-lasting event in the Ancient Olympics.

Instead of the victory going to the driver and horses, all the glory went to the winning owner of the horses and chariot. This made the chariot races very important for wealthy and powerful people. Women were not allowed to compete in the Ancient Olympics but women were allowed to own chariots. Kyniska, daughter of the King of Sparta, decided when she was very young that she wanted to win the chariot races at the Ancient Olympics…and she did. Her horses won twice; they won in 396 BC and 392 BC!

Even though the glory went to the owner, a skilled charioteer did become highly sought after and well rewarded. Karrotos, charioteer for the King of Cyrene, is said to have raced against forty others, all of whom crashed, leaving him unharmed to collect his prize.

My ancient horse relatives who pulled the chariots were greatly honored too. Many horses were bred and raised and trained just for chariot racing. Four mares owned by a man named Kimon want to tell you about being in a race. They were so special that they were buried with Kimon.

We are the four mares owned by Kimon. We won the chariot race
at the Olympics three times! Our driver makes sure we are properly harnessed before the race starts. The two of us in the middle are
harnessed under the yoke and the two outer horses are attached to the
chariot with a rope. The right outer horse is the most important since
the turns are always taken left, the right horse has to be the fastest –
we often reach speeds of forty-five miles per hour during the race! Our
driver, called a charioteer, stands on a wooden-wheeled, open-backed
chariot that rides right on the axle so the ride is very bumpy. The race
is about to begin and we are getting excited! Along with the other
teams that are going to race today we all funnel into a starting gate in
Olympia's specially built stadium for chariot racing called the Hippo-
drome. Eventually, all the chariots and teams of horses will be in the
stadium, hurtling down the track together. The drivers are not allowed
to swerve from their course until they have open track in front of them.
Controlling four powerful horses like us with a whip while cornering at
full speed and attempting to evade a host of rivals out to get you is not
easy but we are very good at obeying the commands of our driver and
we are very fast! Collisions are certain. Locked axles and dropped
whips often lead to flips and smashes. We will race twelve times around
the track, covering about eight and a half miles and we will be   41
victorious!

CHAPTER 14 ~ The Persian Empire and Their Horses

We have learned that in ancient times the rulers of the world were always changing. It didn't take long for the Assyrians to be defeated by the Babylonians then they were defeated by the Persians. We have also seen that great and powerful horses and chariots made for decisive victories.

The Persians had a great ruler named Cyrus he ruled all of the land between Asia Minor and India. He was a good king and kind to the people in the lands that he conquered. In 539 BC Cyrus decided to conquer Babylon too. It was easy because the people of Babylon did not like their king and thought Cyrus would be better so they did not resist. When he took over Babylon, he also took over Canaan where the Jewish people had lived until the Assyrians and Babylonians conquered it and made the Jewish people leave. Cyrus let the Jewish people return to their home and worship their own God.

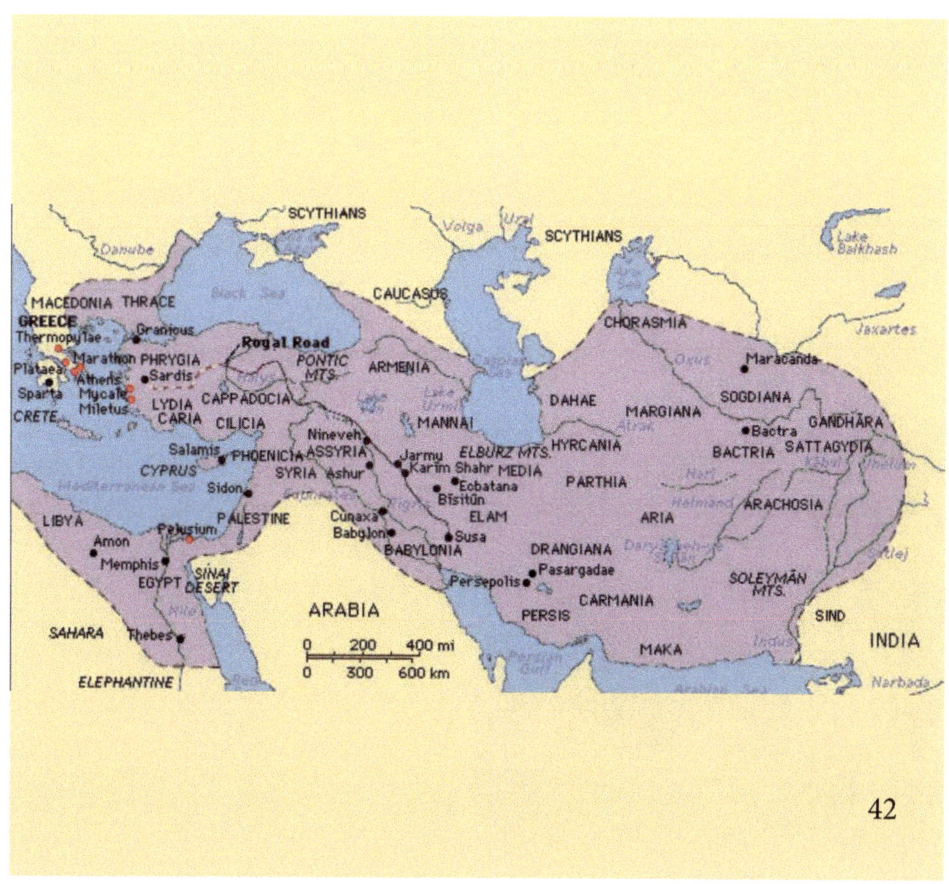

The empire of Cyrus was very big - larger than any previous empire in history. It spanned about three million square miles! They built road systems and even had a postal system. They also had a large professional army. Many people of different origins and faiths and speaking many languages lived in the empire. With such a large, united empire, people were able to learn more about people and inventions from other areas.

We've also learned that rivers and oceans allowed people to travel to different parts of the world but on land, it was travel by horses that linked the vast Persian empire of Cyrus the Great. The Empire of Persia grew to immense power through its use of their very effective cavalry.

Many breeds of horses were used by the Persians as their empire expanded. The governors of the many provinces in the empire provided hundreds of horses from their regions as tribute to their king. The Scythian horses, or ponies, were small and stocky with short manes. Their coats ranged from jet black to light chestnut. The Median horses were very powerful. They had large heads and proud necks. I already told you about the Nisean horses and Cyrus had Nisean horses too. Nisean horses were used for kings and generals to stand out on the battlefield and also demonstrate wealth and authority.

Xenophon was a great Greek cavalry man He wrote books about horses. I'll tell you all about him in the next chapter. He said that the Persians also had a finer horse known as the Armenian horse; now it is called the Caspian horse. It was very small; only about 12 hands. It was fast and agile with small ears and large nostrils

Only chariot horses' manes were kept long. Horses that were ridden had short manes and tied tails to prevent interference from the enemy and weapons. Only the forelock was kept long and, in battle, was tied with a bright ribbon. Persian cavalry soldiers used large, bright, heavily embroidered saddle cloths. The cloth was secured to the horse with breast and girth straps that were knotted around spacers because buckles were still not invented. Stirrups were not invented yet either so it was like riding bareback. The Persian cavalry must have been very good riders. Bridles were made out of soft leather with side straps, nose bands, chinstraps, forehead straps and throat lashes. The bit was made out of iron or bronze.

Xenophon describes the guard of Cyrus the Great as having bronze breastplates and helmets, while their horses wore bronze chamfrons and peitrels together with shoulder pieces which also protected the rider's thighs.

Cyrus was now a very great king but he still had not conquered Greece. Greece was very different than the giant kingdom of Cyrus. Even though in Greece they all worshiped the same gods and spoke the same language, each city had its own army and its own laws. The people who lived in the city of Sparta were strong warriors. All boys left home at the age of seven to learn how to be a soldier. Sparta was ruled by a king who made all the laws. The city of Athens was much different. Athens was a democracy and rather then being ruled by a king, the people were allowed to vote for the laws they wanted. Since they were given the right to vote, education was very important to the people of Athens. Sometimes the cities did   44
not get along and would fight with each other.

The Persians decided they wanted to rule Greece too so they sent messengers to Greece asking them to surrender. The Geeks could not believe that they were being asked to surrender their cities. They chose to fight instead so the many cites of Greece united against the Persians. The war lasted a very long time; it lasted from 500 BC until 480 BC and eventually the Greeks won and did not become part of the Persian empire.

Sometimes while kings were out waging war, people at home would try to take over and become the ruler. There was a time in Persia when there were many conflicts among people about who would be the leader of Persia. Eventually all of their plots to take over backfired and the Persian empire was without a leader. The people who caused all of the problems had to decide the future of the empire. Being unable to settle the matter, all of them agreed on a contest, where the winner would take the throne. All of them would meet the next morning, each on his horse, and the first horse to neigh at the sunrise would be named the new king. Some people think that Darius cheated; supposedly it was his servant, Oebares, who made the horse neigh by letting the animal smell his hand that he had previously rubbed on a mare. In any case, the horse's neigh accompanied by lightning and thunder from a storm convinced the others to accept Darius as the new king. Pretty amazing that a horse decided who the ruler of Persia would be! Darius the Great, was the third Persian King. His reign lasted 36 years, from 522 BC to 486 BC. During this time the Persian Empire reached its peak.

CHAPTER 15 ~ Xenophon and Horsemanship

Xenophon knew a lot about horses. He was born in Athens in 430 BC. Xenophon was an author and also a military leader of the Greek mercenary army. A mercenary is a professional soldier hired to serve in a foreign army. The Persians knew that they could conquer Greece because the Greek city states did not get along with each other so all they had to do was prod them into war among themselves. Xenophon was one of the leaders of the Ten Thousand Greeks recruited by Cyrus the Younger, son of Cyrus the Great, to fight for Persia. Unfortunately, Cyrus was killed in the unsuccessful attempt to conquer Greece. Xenophon fought in many battles and even sent his sons to Sparta to be educated.

Xenophon is well known for his writings about the world he lived in at the time. He wrote a lot about Athens, Sparta, Persians, generals and kings, as well as horses and dogs. All of his writings survive to the present day. Since most of his experiences involved battles, it makes sense that two of his books would be about horses. "On Horsemanship" is all about owning and riding horses and "On the Cavalry Commander" is about how to improve the Athenian cavalry corps.

Xenophon was the first person to teach people to respect a horse and to get to know the horse so that horse and human could communicate with each other in a good way. Many people today still use some of the methods taught by Xenophon. Isn't it amazing to think that my ancient horse relatives and your ancient human relatives learned the same things 46
we are learning now.

This is what he wrote in his book, "On Horsemanship":

"The one great precept and practice in using a horse is this – never deal with him when you are in a fit of passion. When your horse shies at an object and is unwilling to go up to it, he should be shown that there is nothing fearful in it, least of all to a courageous horse like him; but if this fails, touch the object yourself that seems so dreadful to him, and lead him up to it with gentleness. Compulsion and blows inspire only the more fear; and when horses are at all hurt at such times, they think what they shied at is the cause of the hurt."

Remember that we learned that the cities of Greece often warred with each other. At the time that Xenophon wrote "On the Cavalry Commander" war loomed between two Greek cities, Thebes and Athens. They had been at peace for some time so Athens was suffering from a decline in the quality of its cavalry. Xenophon hoped his advice on how to restore the cavalry to its previous excellence would help them become great again. Xenophon realized the effectiveness of the horse in war. He knew that the best war horse had to be bred, trained and treated very carefully. He encouraged the idea that kindness was, in fact, the method that achieved the most positive results from the horses.

Have you ever heard of Alexander the Great and his magnificent horse Bucephalus? Many people who study history think that Alexander the Great read many of Xenophon's books and that Xenophon was a large reason Alexander had so much skill in handling horses.

Now I'm going to tell you about Alexander the Great and Bucephalus.

CHAPTER 16 ~ Alexander the Great and Bucephalus

The Greek cities states were so busy fighting among themselves and having battles that soon none of the armies of the city states were powerful. That made it easy for Greece to be invaded.

Philip was a ruler in Macedonia. He saw how weak Greece was and easily conquered Greece. Philip was the first person to have the idea of a cavalry charge. Until then, mounted soldiers fought in a scattered, disorganized way, each doing whatever he and his horse were able to do according to his skill and his horse's skill. Philip demanded that his horsemen drill for their massed cavalry charges. Philip's ideas for how to successfully use horses was a big reason why he was able to conquer so many lands. Philip's son, Alexander, became an even greater soldier and leader than his father. At only eighteen, in 338 BC, Alexander fought at his father's side at the Battle of Chaeronea.

In the summer of 336 BC, Philip was home in Macedonia celebrating a family wedding and his upcoming invasion of Asia. Philip ordered his bodyguards to leave him for a time. Pausanias, one of Philip's guards, disobeyed those orders and lingered behind. Unnoticed, he plunged a dagger into Philip, killing him. To this day, no one really knows who plotted Philip's murder. Alexander acted quickly though to secure his power and to make sure he would become his father's successor.

After Philip's assassination, Alexander continued to make the cavalry great. His work paid off because Alexander established the largest 48 empire the ancient world had ever seen.

First Alexander forced the Greek city states to acknowledge his authority.
Like his father, he wanted to conquer the great empire of Persia. Alexander
advanced gradually and conquered Persia territory by territory. Darius, the
Great King of Persia, was murdered by conspirators soon afterward. Then
Alexander conquered Phoenicia, Egypt and Babylon. Alexander went on
to conquer the Paraetacene territory. In the Far East, Alexander founded
a large number of cities that would contribute to the expansion of Greek
culture.

Finally, there remained India - which at the time referred to a small area
in western Pakistan, not the country of modern times. It was a frightful
expedition since the cavalry had to battle elephants but still, Alexander
was victorious.

After India, Alexander wanted to keep going but by now his army was
tired and wanted to go home after eight hard years of combat and march-
ing. Alexander was furious, but he was eventually forced to give in and
return home. So, Alexander went home and ruled his empire until his
death from a fever at age thirty-two in 323 BC. After he died his generals
divided his empire into three kingdoms.

Bucephalus was Alexander the Great's horse and many people think that he is the most famous horse in history.

Alexander and Bucephalus' first meeting showed why Alexander became one of the greatest generals in all of history.

Bucephalus was brought to Macedonia and presented to Alexander's father, Philip in 346 BC by Philoneicus of Thessaly. The price for Bucephalus was three times what any other horse at the time would cost. He was magnificent! The beautiful black horse stood taller than the normal Macedonian horses but he was considered too wild. He was rearing up against anyone who came near him so Philip ordered him led away.

Alexander sat in the audience watching the horse. As the attendants tried to lead Bucephalus away, Alexander rose calling them cowardly and said, "What an excellent horse do they lose for want of address and boldness to manage him!" At first Philip ignored his son but finally said to Alexander, "Do you reproach those who are older than yourself, as if you were better able to manage him than they?" Alexander, ignoring his father's remark, repeated his challenge and said he would pay for the horse if he, Alexander, were unable to tame him.

Amid wild laughter, Alexander approached the horse calmly. He had realized something the others had not - the horse was afraid of his own shadow. Turning the horse toward the sun, so his shadow was behind him, and slowly taking the reins in his hand, Alexander mounted him. The laughter of the crowd turned to cheers as Alexander rode off. Alexander named him Bucephalus and he became Alexander's favorite horse. At one point, Bucephalus was stolen and Alexander promised to lay waste to the land and kill the inhabitants if the horse was not returned — which, of course, he promptly was.

CHAPTER 17 ~ The Known World is Getting Bigger

We learned that the early people who lived on Earth were nomads. They did not have a way to travel to other parts of the world other than on foot or by traveling on rivers. People in the world at the time did not know about other places or other people who lived in the world. They did not know about inventions discovered by other people in the world and they knew nothing of cultures other than their own. But when people learned to harness the power of the horse all of that changed! People could now travel further and faster. Horse drawn chariots changed the face of the world as they rumbled through Greece, Asia Minor, Iran, India and China. People learned about other cultures and cultures intermingled. Inventions and ideas began to spread to many parts of the world.

ALL BECAUSE OF THE HORSE!

We have learned about Assyrians, Babylonians, Israelites, Greeks, Egyptians and Persians. The rulers of the world were always changing.

Alexander's Empire was very big but there was an Empire that was even bigger and lasted even longer than Alexander's empire. It was the Roman Empire. The Roman Empire lasted five hundred years! I have so much to tell you about the Roman Empire….and of course…. horses.

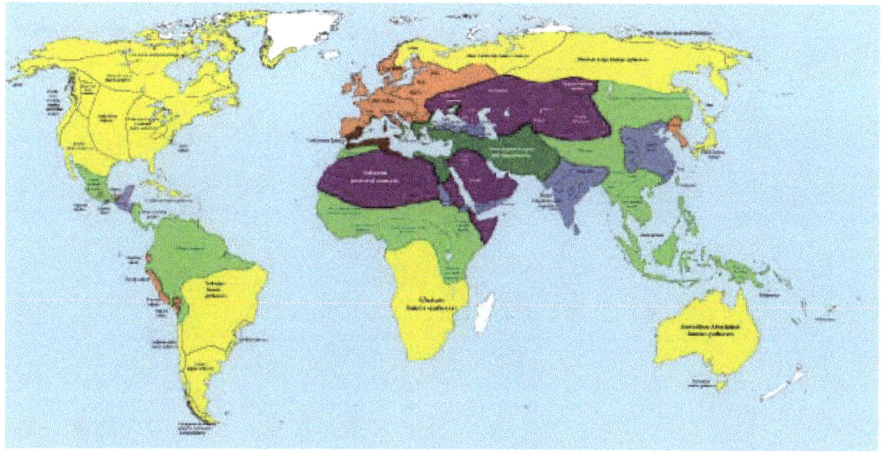

World Map 323 BC

Rome is a city in Italy. If you visit Rome you can see the ruins of many of the buildings of ancient Rome. There were many statues of horses in ancient Rome. Ancient sources tell us that there were twenty-two "equi magni"—colossal bronze equestrian statues—that decorated the imperial capital. The statue of Marcus Aurelius is the only one left standing today. The other twenty-one equi magni were melted down during times of war or strife. Isn't it sad that statues are destroyed? It is such an important way to learn about history.

This single statue was preserved because it was incorrectly identified as the later emperor Constantine, who reigned from 306 AD to 337 AD. To later Christians, Constantine was an important historic figure so the statue was not melted down.

The statue of the magnificent rider and his horse display power and nobility, as if they are still riding through the streets of Rome today. Even though they incorrectly identified the person on the horse, people knew the person was important because he was on a horse. People knew that horses were a sign of power, strength, wealth and importance.

These huge statues of horses and riders displayed messages of dominance, power, and virtue through strength. Roman equestrian statues were about much more than men with horses; they represented the relationship between the leader and the military. The equites, a military class, played an incredibly important role in Roman society. The equites received positions of privilege through merit and imperial favor instead of through a noble bloodline. We'll learn about them later. They were very powerful people.

The statue does not explain the history of Roman rule but it sure makes it seem like Rome must have been pretty amazing. Let's learn more about Rome.

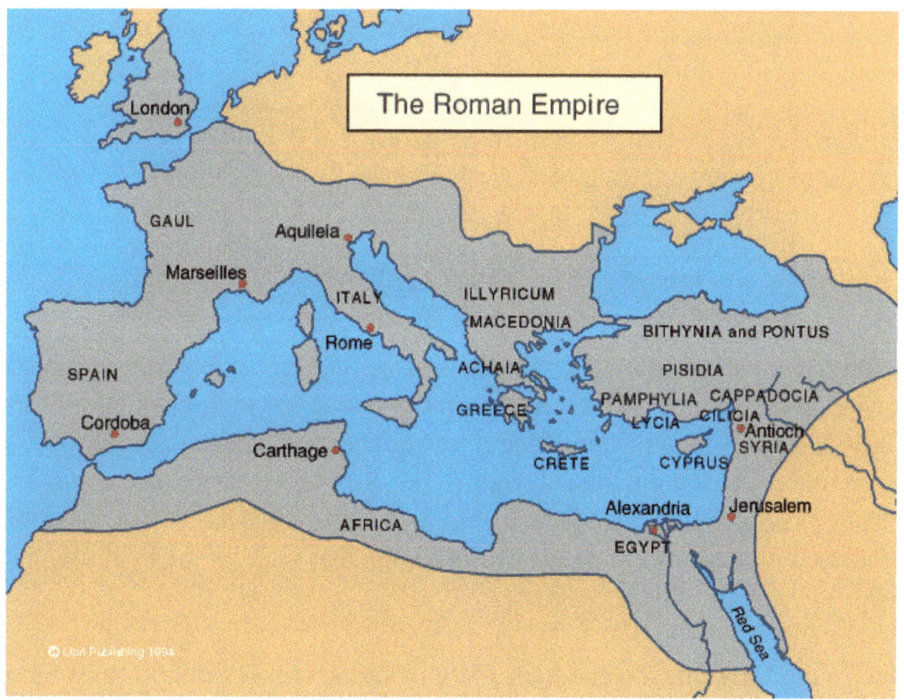

CHAPTER 19 ~ The Roman Republic

Ancient Rome had two major periods of history. The first was the Roman Republic which lasted from 509 BC to 27 BC. During this time there was no single leader of Rome. The government was run by elected officials.

The second period was the Roman Empire which lasted from 27 BC to 476 AD. During this time the government was led by an emperor. The Roman Republic eventually collapsed as a result of internal problems, unlike the Roman Empire which collapsed as a result of external threats.

Rome was a small city state in the sixth century BC and was governed by kings. After only seven kings had ruled the city, the people who lived there managed to overthrow the kings and create a republic form of government that would represent the wishes of the Roman citizens. A senate was put in place to rule over Rome.

In 450 BC the first Roman law code was written on twelve bronze tablets–known as the Twelve Tables–and publicly displayed in the Roman Forum. These laws included issues of legal procedure, civil rights and property rights and provided the basis for all future Roman civil law. By around 300 BC, real political power in Rome was centered in the Senate, which at the time included only members of patrician and wealthy plebeian families.

Once Rome became a republic it grew in strength and went on to conquer much of the Mediterranean. Rome's military conquests led to its cultural growth as a society. The Romans benefited greatly from contact with such advanced cultures as the Greeks.

In late July 390 BC, Rome fell to Celtic invaders from Gaul who burnt and sacked the city. The Romans considered the Celts to be barbarians. Their long hair and mustaches were strange looking to the Romans. They were fearsome fighters and just plain scary in action and deed as well. This was the first time that the Romans encountered the Celtic cavalry. The horsemen of the Celtic cavalry had most likely been riding since childhood. Thousands of fearless and yelling horsemen invaded a stunned Rome. On the Capitol Hill a small number of Romans put up a valiant defense, holding out until famine forced them to surrender. The Romans were forced to pay the Gauls a large ransom of gold to depart. The Gauls too had been overcome by starvation and by malaria.

Gaul sacks Rome 390 BC

To prevent their city from being sacked again, the Romans improved their military and strengthened the city wall and became powerful under the leadership of the military hero Camillus. Rome eventually gained control of the entire Italian peninsula by 264 BC.

Rome then fought a series of wars known as the Punic Wars with Carthage, a powerful city-state in northern Africa. In 219 BC, Hannibal of Carthage led an attack on Saguntum, an independent city in the middle of the eastern Spanish coast that was allied with Rome. This sparked the outbreak of the Second Punic War. Hannibal then assembled a massive army of ninety thousand infantry, twelve thousand cavalry and nearly forty elephants. They marched one thousand miles through the Pyrenees, across the Rhone River and the snowcapped Alps, and finally into central Italy. After a string of victories, Hannibal gained a foothold in southern Italy, but declined to mount an attack on Rome itself.

In 203 BC, Hannibal abandoned the struggle in Italy so that he could defend North Africa instead. A treaty concluded the Second Punic War so now Rome was in full control of Sicily, the western Mediterranean and much of Spain. Even though the treaty put an end to the war, Hannibal continued to pursue his lifelong dream of destroying Rome up until his death in 183 BC.

The Macedonian Wars began during the Second Punic War when Philip of Macedon allied with Hannibal. The city-states of Greece were under the influence of the Macedonians. The Achaean League, a group of Greek city states wanted Greek independence. Sometimes they allied with Rome and sometimes they opposed Rome. In Rome, many people were great admirers of Greek culture and learning while some thought that the Greeks were corrupt. After Rome won the Second Punic War, they launched an expedition to Macedonia in order to prevent Philip V from making further alliances unfriendly to Rome. Many of the Greek city states joined in an alliance with Rome against Macedonia. It was a decisive victory for the Romans. The Romans imposed severe restrictions on Philip V's foreign policy, and "freed" the Greek cities from Macedonian control.

In the Third Punic War (149 BC– 146 B.C.), the Romans captured and destroyed the city of Carthage. All of the inhabitants were enslaved and the city destroyed. A curse was set on any person who attempted to resettle the area. North Africa was then made a Roman province while the cities who had been loyal to Rome were given the privilege of freedom from tax. Carthage would remain uninhabited until the city was re-founded by Julius Caesar.

Horses, elephants, armies - the world is changing and cultures are min-gling! The Roman Republic is about to become the Roman Empire.

Despite the power of Rome, most people who lived in Italy were still afraid of invasions from Gaul.

Gaul is the name given by the Romans to the territories where the Celtic Gauls lived. The people who lived there were made up of a multitude of states of different ethnic origin. Gaul included present day France, Belgium, Luxemburg and parts of the Netherlands, Switzerland, Germany on the west bank of the Rhine, and the Po Valley in present Italy.

The horses of Gaul were small compared to those of Italy. Horse-breeding was an important part of Celtic culture. Horses were used both for riding and as pack animals. Trade and commerce increased throughout Gaul thanks to the use of the horses and eventually the different cultures of the many states of Gaul started to mingle and become one culture. Eventually people from Germany started to migrate into Gaul. The people in Italy were afraid of the Gauls but they were terrified of the Germans! The Germans were fearless in battle. In battle, a swift German light infantry soldier ran alongside each cavalryman, clinging to the horse's mane to keep pace. He protected the cavalryman's flanks and stabbed at the enemy horse.

The Roman Republic stood strong for several centuries. However, as Rome's power and territory expanded, internal wars, called civil wars, began to arise as citizens and families fought among themselves for power. During these civil wars, an important general and statesmen named Julius Caesar began gaining much power. He commanded the loyalty of the soldiers in his army. Julius Caesar decided to end the threat from   59
Gaul and conquer the territory.

In his conquest of Gaul, Julius Caesar relied on the magnificent horses and riders of Gaul and Germany. It was not unusual for those who felt looming defeat to join the army of the conqueror. Caesar valued these warriors. Time and time again they lead Caesar to victory on their small but mighty horses.

Caesar's conquest of Gaul made him very powerful. The Senate in Rome became fearful of Caesar's power and demanded he give up command of his army and return to Rome as a citizen. Caesar refused and instead marched his army south directly into Rome. As a result, another civil war broke out between Caesar and his chief political rival, Pompey. Caesar was victorious, and was named dictator for life. Other leaders within the Republic feared Caesar would become a tyrant with this new title. To prevent this, a group of senators conspired and assassinated him on March 15, 44 BC. Marc Antony was Caesar's second in command. He heard rumors of a plot against Caesar but was unable to warn him in time. Antony fled Rome dressed as a slave but soon returned to protect his friend's legacy from the senators who had conspired against him. He took charge of Caesar's will and papers and gave a stirring eulogy for the fallen leader.

Assassination of Julius Caesar March 15, 44 BC

We already learned that the Chinese invented many things. The Romans are also well known for their many innovations. In ancient times Rome and China were able to learn about each other and trade with each other. They are so far apart! How and why did this happen? Trade routes and horses of course.

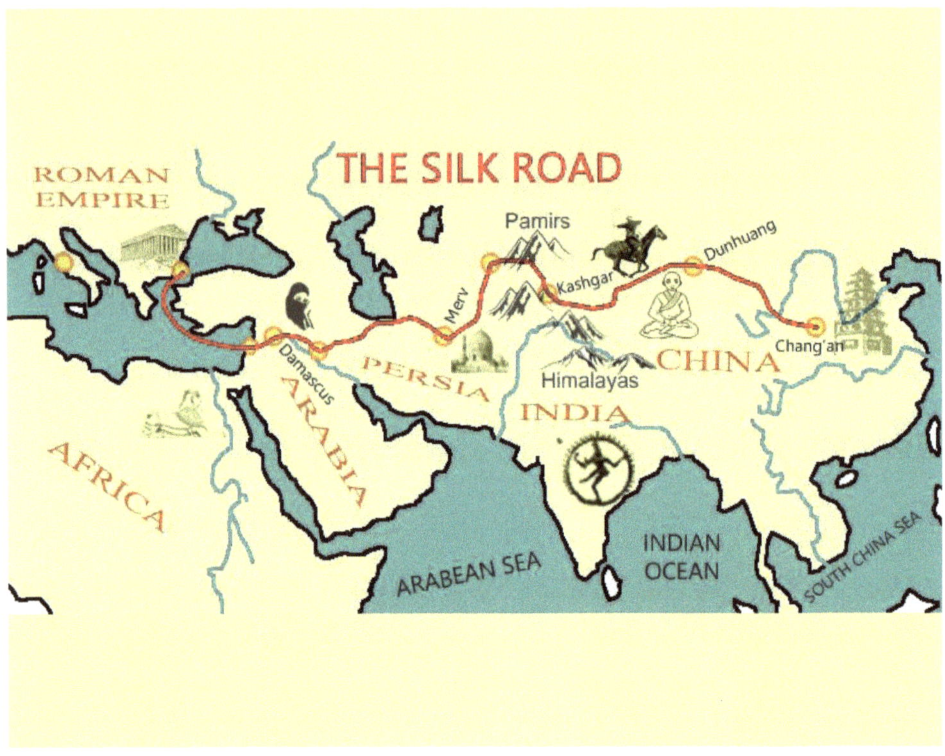

The art of turning the cocoons of the silkworm moth into shimmering fabric was discovered by the Chinese. They kept the method a secret and soldiers inspected the baggage of merchants to make sure they were not smuggling silkworms or cocoons out of the country. The fabric made from the silk was exported and in great demand. These silken threads wove together a vast trade network, linking the lands of China to Rome. Goods traveled thousands of miles in both directions via the "Silk Road". The Silk Road wasn't actually a road. It was a trade route. It was a major trade route from 130 BC to 1453 AD. Merchants only journeyed along short sections. When they reached the next city, they would sell their merchandise to the locals, who then would travel along the next segment and trade with the merchants there. Can you see how cultures began to mingle?

How do you think people transported the goods on the Silk Road? Horses and camels played an important role in the silk road transportation. The Chinese however were unsuccessful in breeding horses themselves for many centuries and tried to buy or trade for horses.

In 138 BC, General Zhang Qian, the commander of the guards at the imperial palace, volunteered to make the dangerous journey to Central Asia to make peace with nomadic tribes in order to trade silk for their horses. General Zhang set off with a hundred mounted men. They were ambushed and captured and remained in captivity for ten years.

Dayuan was a country in the Ferghana valley in Central Asia. They possessed the most amazing horses known to the Chinese at the time. They were called Heavenly Horses. When General Zhang Qian saw the horses they had he was stunned by their beauty and strength. They stood sixteen hands and were superior in muscle and stamina to China's horses. The general finally managed to escape and return to the Han court. He described the magnificent steeds to the Emperor.

During the continual wars among growing empires in Asia, achieving power depended on the ability to fight on horseback. The art of cavalry required the strongest horses. Emperor Wu Di wanted to trade bolts of silk for a thousand horses and march them back along the northern Silk Road to the Han court. However, it was easier said than done. The horses were considered national treasures so the Dayuan refused to trade or even sell the horses. They even confiscated the gold sent as payment for the horses.

So began the first war ever fought over horses. It was called the War of the Heavenly Horses.

Rare polychrome pottery
Ferghana horse (heavenly horse)
Tang Dynasty 618-907)

62

Wu Di was mad and wanted those horses! He sent out Li Guangli with six thousand horsemen and twenty thousand infantry soldiers. Li's army had to cross the Taklamakan Desert and his supplies soon ran out. After a gruesome march of over one thousand miles, he finally arrived to the country of Dayuan, but what remained of his army was exhausted and starving. After a severe defeat at a place called Yucheng, Li concluded that he was not strong enough to take the enemy capital and therefore returned home in 102 BC. Emperor Wu Di then gave Li Guangli a much larger army along with a huge number of oxen, donkeys and camels to carry supplies. With this force he had no difficulty reaching Dayuan this time. After a forty day siege, the Chinese had broken through the outer wall and cut off the water supply. The people of Dayuan eventually offered the Chinese all the horses they wanted. Li accepted the offer and went back home with three thousand horses.

New research shows that Silk Road trading helped to produce the modern horse. DNA research today has shown that ancient Silk Road commerce caused population mixing in horses as far as five thousand miles apart. Isn't that remarkable?! Do you think I'm related to horses that traveled the Silk Road?

The horse in this picture is an Akhal-Teke horse. Akhal-Teke horses are the breed that is believed to be descendants of the Heavenly Horses. In 2014 the Turkmenistan President gave one to President Xi Jinping of China. Turkmenistan has traditionally given Akhal-Teke horses to China's new presidents after they take office. The horse was even trained to bow on one knee when it was given to the President.

Rome was not so sure they liked the idea of trade with China and importing so much silk. Pliny the Elder, a Roman author wrote: "At least a hundred million sesterces (a large brass coin) flow out of our empire every year to India, China and Arabia. That is how much luxury and women cost us!"

Rome, which was considered to be "The West", also had wonderful things to trade back to "The East". The Roman empire was very large and they had a system of roads to connect their empire that made trading very profitable.

The first major Roman road was the Appian Way. It was built in 312 BC and is still in existence today! It served as the main highway to the seaports of southeastern Italy and thus to Greece and the eastern Mediterranean.

Road systems often sprang up after Roman conquest of a region. The Romans built new highways to link captured cities with Rome and establish them as colonies. The Roman road system was made up of about fifty thousand miles stretching from Syria in the east to Britain in the west. Caesar once covered eight hundred miles in ten days on one of the Roman roads. A person on horseback could cover three hundred sixty miles in two and a half days. Horse and mule carts averaged five to six miles per hour. This speed of transportation remained unequaled until the nineteenth century!

Roman roads were very easy to travel; they had road signs and mile markers. They also had state-run hotels and way stations. The most common of these ancient rest stops were the horse changing stations which were located every ten miles along most routes. These simple post houses consisted of stables where government travelers could trade their winded horse or donkey for a fresh mount.

64

From West to East the goods traded over the centuries were:
• Horses
• Saddles and Riding Tack
• The grapevine and grapes
• Dogs and other animals both exotic and domestic
• Animal furs and skins
• Honey
• Fruits
• Glassware
• Woolen blankets, rugs, carpets
• Textiles (such as curtains)
• Gold and Silver
• Slaves
• Weapons and armor

From East to West the goods traded over the centuries were:
• Silk
• Tea
• Dyes
• Precious Stones
• China (plates, bowls, cups, vases)
• Porcelain
• Spices (such as cinnamon and ginger)
• Bronze and gold artifacts
• Medicine
• Perfumes
• Ivory
• Rice
• Paper
• Gunpowder

CHAPTER 22 ~ The Importance of Rivers – in a New Way!

We learned that early people lived near rivers so that they could have water to drink and grow their crops. The Roman Empire had many cities that were not near rivers. If the Roman Empire relied on only building cities near rivers it would restrict their potential growth. They needed to figure out a way to get water to the people who lived in the cites. Since Rome was a military empire, the horse was an essential element in communications, transport and fighting. The empire was vast and wherever the army went, the horses needed to be fed and watered too. How did they get water to all of the places that were not near rivers?

The solution was aqueducts. Aqueducts are a complex network of ground works, pipes and other structures designed to transfer water from a source to a destination. Rome's aqueducts supported a population of over a million. Once built, aqueducts had to be maintained and protected. The excellent planning of the ancient Romans made sure that maintenance requirements were part of the plans. Repair people could get to underground sections of the aqueducts by means of manholes and shafts. They even had a way to divert water away from a damaged section until it was repaired. Some of the aqueducts are still in use today.

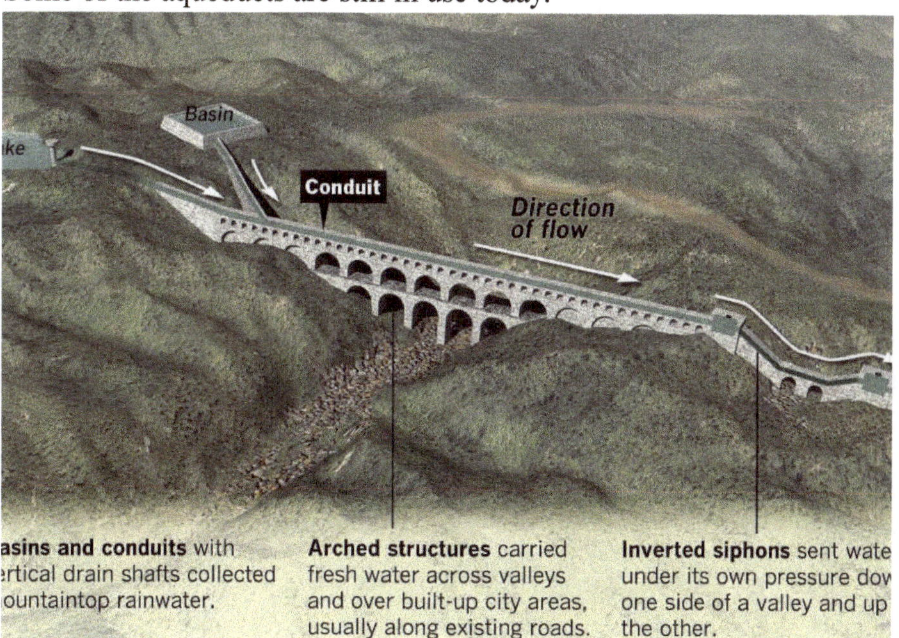

asins and conduits with ertical drain shafts collected ountaintop rainwater.

Arched structures carried fresh water across valleys and over built-up city areas, usually along existing roads.

Inverted siphons sent wate under its own pressure dov one side of a valley and up the other.

Until recently, excavations have not found any stables in Roman forts.
Does that mean that the army stayed in the forts and they kept the horses
near rivers so that they could get water? That would not be efficient. By
the time they got to the horses it may be too late to save the city. In 1998
-2000 excavations found that soldiers and horses actually lived together in
the same building. There was a natural bond between these mounted warriors and their horses. The soldier and his mount rode together and lived
together in a tight-knit community, realizing that, as Xenophon advised,
"It is plain that in danger the master entrusts his life to his horse."

This is a picture of the excavation of a Roman fort. The stone walls outline
where the barracks would have been. Horses lived in the grassy area in the
middle. The long pit collected horse urine and would have been covered
with boards or stone slabs to keep the floor dry.

CHAPTER 23 ~ The Roman Republic Becomes the Roman Empire

After the assassination of Julius Caesar his nephew, and adopted heir, Octavian, joined forces with Consul Marc Antony to crush Brutus and Cassius, the ones responsible for Caesar's assassination. The victors divided power in Rome with Octavian leading the western provinces, Antony the east, and Lepidus, another consul, leading Africa. The Senate persuaded Marc Antony to marry Octavian's sister, Octavia, in order to keep peace among the leaders of the regions.

Cleopatra was the Egyptian queen at the time. She was clever and well educated. Marc Antony fell in love with Cleopatra and developed a political alliance with her. In 32 BC Antony divorced Octavia. In revenge, Octavian declared war, not on Antony but on Cleopatra. As Octavian entered Alexandria, both Antony and Cleopatra resolved to commit suicide. After Antony's death his honors were all revoked, his statues removed and no one in the dead general's family was ever allowed to have the name Marc Antony again. In 27 BC Octavian assumed the title of Augustus and became the first emperor of Rome. After four hundred fifty years as a republic, Rome became an empire.

Augustus

Augustus' rule was a time of peace after all of the civil wars. Roman literature, art, architecture and religion began to flourish. Augustus ruled for fifty-six years with the support of his great army. The citizens of Rome developed a cult-like devotion to the emperor. When he died, the Senate elevated Augustus to the status of a god.

68

Rome had peace and prosperity for two centuries. This time was known as the Pax Romana.

At its peak the Roman empire included most of mainland Europe, Britain, much of western Asia, northern Africa and the Mediterranean islands. The legacy of the Roman empire includes the widespread use of the Romance languages (Italian, French, Spanish, Portuguese and Romanian), the modern Western alphabet, the calendar and the rise of Christianity as a major world religion.

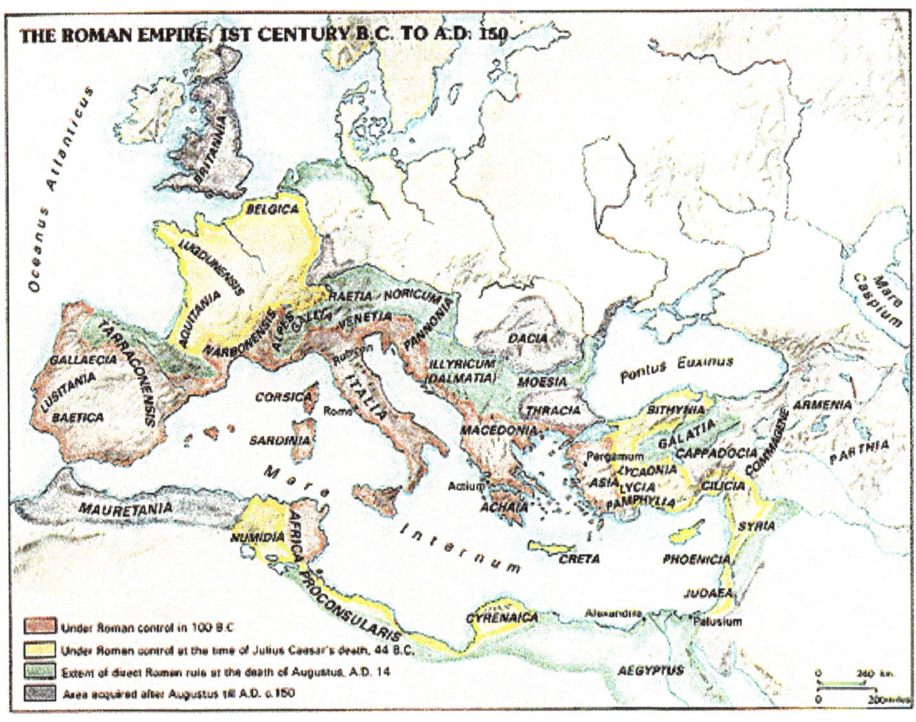

Outside the major cities of the Roman Empire people lived a simple life on farms, dependent almost entirely on their own labor. The countryside played an important role in the economy of the Roman Empire. Many different foods were grown in different areas and then shipped throughout the empire.

One of the most important crops was grain. A lot of grains were grown in Egypt and then shipped to large cities such as Rome. The city of Rome had to import around six million sacks of grain each year to feed its large population. Other major crops of the Roman Empire included grapes for making wine and olives for olive oil. Olives were grown in Spain and North Africa and then imported to Rome. How do you think all of these goods were transported in the Roman Empire? Although transport by sea was the cheapest and fastest method it could also be the most dangerous. Often there were thefts from pirates and the weather from November to March was too unsafe for travel by sea. We've already learned that Roman roads were very easy to travel; they had road signs and mile markers. They also had state-run hotels and way stations. Many rest stops had stables where government travelers could trade their winded horse or donkey for a fresh mount. Horses played an important part in transporting goods through the empire.

Life in the cites was much different. People moved to cites looking for jobs and hopefully a better way of life. Like today, cities also offered more things for people to do. Most cites were made up of a mix of many cultures; Greeks, Syrians, Jews, North Africans, Spaniards, Gauls and Britons. For the affluent, the day was divided between business and leisure. Business was only conducted in the morning. Most Romans worked a six-hour day, beginning at dawn and ending at noon, and some shops reopened in the early evening.

The afternoon was devoted to leisure - attending the games the theater or the baths - all of which were also enjoyed by the poor because many in government felt the need for the poor to be entertained. Even during times of crises, the citizens of Rome were kept happy with games. What kinds of games did they play? Did they have Monopoly back then? The "games" that entertained the Romans were spectator events. The people of Rome went to the Colosseum and the Circus Maximus for the games.

Measuring six hundred twenty feet by five hundred thirteen feet, the Colosseum was the largest amphitheater in the Roman world and was in use for four hundred years. Many earlier amphitheaters were dug into hillsides to provide adequate support but, the Colosseum in Rome was a freestanding structure made of stone and concrete. The Colosseum had seating for as many as eighty thousand spectators with free admission and food for all visitors. The emperors were always at the games and sometimes they even participated.

Events at the Colosseum lasted from dawn until sundown and began with a grand entrance of competitors in chariots with horses. The "games" included fights between gladiators. Next there were dangerous animals such as lions, tigers, bears, elephants, leopards, hippopotamuses and bulls that condemned criminals had to fight. The Romans would often re-enact famous military victories too. They would even fill the Colosseum with water and reenact naval battles!

The Colosseum was certainly a place with amazing events. Are you wondering what they did in the Circus Maximus? Did they have a circus in the Circus Maximus?

The Circus Maximus was a chariot racetrack in Rome. It was originally built in the sixth century BC. It was also used to host the Roman Games (Ludi Romani) which honored the god Jupiter. These were held every September with 15 days of chariot races and military processions. The Circus Maximus had room for two hundred fifty thousand spectators!

The Circus Maximus had:

• a track covered in sand about the length of five football fields.
• twelve starting gates for chariots at the open end of the track.
• a decorated barrier called a spina complete with obelisks running down the center of the track.
• tapering turning posts placed at each end of the track.
• lap markers in the shape of eggs and dolphins which were turned to mark the completion of each of the seven circuits of a typical race.

Charioteers were like our movie stars today. They were very popular and became very rich. The most famous charioteer was Scorpus; he won two thousand races!

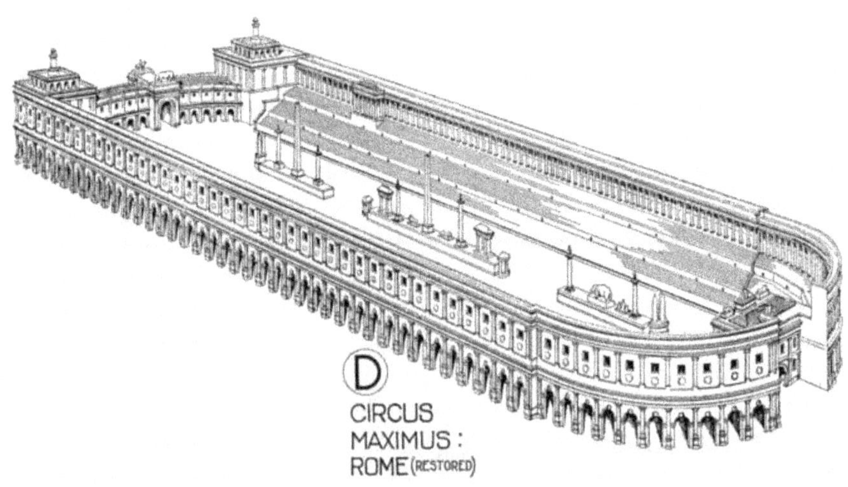

Although there were individual stars, there were four main teams named after the colors they wore – the Reds, Whites, Blues and Greens. People had much loyalty to their teams; much like football today. At hockey games today, some spectators throw things on the ice - even though it is not allowed. At the chariot races, spectators were encouraged to sabotage the opposing team by throwing lead amulets studded with nails at the racers. As you can imagine, clashes between supporters of opposing teams happened often.

Horses became famous too. Just like the Kentucky Derby today, horses for the chariot races were specially bred. Race horses were bred and trained on private and later imperial farms. When ancient Roman records mentioned horse breeds the Numidian breed was mentioned most frequently. Other breeds used were the Spanish horses. The training of a race horse would begin about the age of five and their careers could last up to twenty years. After their racing careers, if they were successful, they were used for breeding.

The chariots were pulled by teams of four, six, eight or twelve horses. The lead horse in a chariot race was often as famous or more famous than the driver. Fans knew the breeding line and all the details of their favorite horses.

Teams of four horses were called a quadriga, meaning four yoked. The two outside horses were called the funalis and the two middle ones were the iguales, or the actual yoke horses. The funalis were the faster horses who would set the pace, while the iguales were the ones who pulled the weight of chariot and kept it steady. All the horses would need to work as a team and match pace with each other and take signals from their driver on when to slow down and when to speed up. A bad horse would have spelled disaster for the whole team. The inside funalis horse was the one closest to the spina; he had the most difficult job because he had to lead the team around the sharp turns while keeping the fast pace.

When a specific horse was named in a quadriga in ancient records, it would usually be the inside funalis horse. Some of the names of hero race horses were: Abigieus, Lucidus, Cotynus, Galata, Pompeianus. The names mean nothing to us now, of course, but the mere mention in the stadium of "Abigieus" would drive the people crazy.

Horses needed to be very strong and fast and agile too. They needed enough speed to gallop the straightaways and still be able to negotiate the dangerous turns at the turning posts; that is where most chariots would overturn. The chariot, driver and horses had to complete seven full laps around the Circus Maximus for a total of about four miles.

In later years of the Roman Empire, the Roman emperor Caligula owned a retired, unbeaten chariot horse named Incitatus.

Incitatus had a stable made of marble and a stall made of ivory. He wore only purple blankets, the color of royalty, and had jewels hanging from around his neck. The horse had its own servants and its oats were mixed with gold flakes. The emperor would issue invitations, on the horse's behalf, inviting dignitaries to dinners attended by the horse's servants and would host lavish birthday parties in the horse's honor.

Do you remember Cyrus the Great? He built the empire of Persia. Then Alexander the Great conquered the whole Persian Empire, Asia Minor and the entire coast line from Greece to Egypt, Mesopotamia, Media and parts of modern Afghanistan, Pakistan and parts of the Steppes of central Asia. He conquered almost the entire earth known to the Greeks at that time! Alexander left Greeks in charge wherever he went. The colonies he set up were called Hellenistic colonies. Hellenistic refers to the spread of Greek language, culture and population into the areas conquered by Alexander. His next conquest would be India. We already learned that India is where Alexander ended his conquest of the world. Let's learn more about India.

The history of India tells a story of constant mingling of people with the diverse cultures that surrounded India. The earliest people in India were farmers who lived by rivers – just like the rest of the world. The Vedic civilization is the earliest civilization in the history of ancient India. It flourished between 1500 BC and 500 BC. This civilization was the foundation of Hinduism.

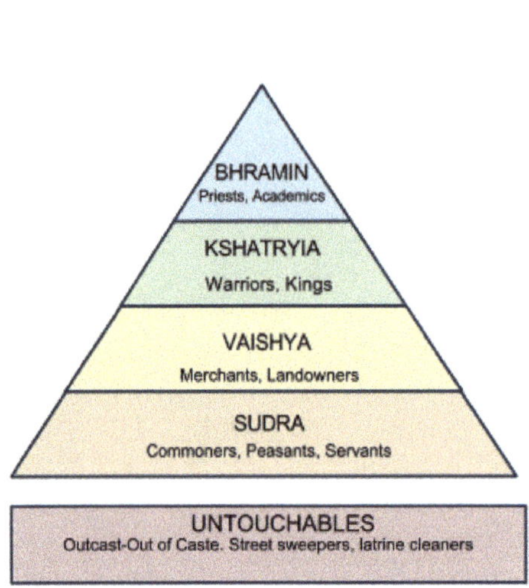

Indians lived by a caste system. There were four castes of people. If you were a farmer you would always be a farmer and could only marry a farmer. Then there were the very poor people who did not belong to a caste at all; they were called the untouchables. They were only allowed to be out at night and a Hindu believed if they touched one, they would become unclean.

Buddha was born in 560 BC and died at the age of eighty in 480 BC. Buddha, whose original name was Siddhartha Gautama, was the founder of Buddhism. He grew up in a palace and wanted to learn about the world outside of his palace. When he went on his journey of discovery, he was shocked to find that some people, like the untouchables, suffered so much. He thought long and hard about life and determined that all people can find happiness if they lead a good life. From then on Siddhartha was known as the Buddha. His followers became known as Buddhists. The religion and the philosophical system of Buddhism became a great culture throughout much of southern and eastern Asia.

In 326 BC, Alexander invaded India. The Indians were defeated in a fierce battle, even though they fought with elephants, which Alexander's army had never before seen. The horses in his army were not accustomed to the sight of elephants. An elephant can charge at twenty-five miles per hour. Imagine how much the horses were frightened by the charging elephants. But Alexander knew the weak points of an elephant and had prepared his cavalry. Again – horses played an important part in history!

Alexander captured King Porus and, like the other local rulers he had defeated, allowed him to continue to govern his territory. During his time in India Alexander sought out the Indian philosophers, the Brahmins, who were famous for their wisdom. They were members of the highest Hindu caste, that of the priesthood. Alexander debated with them on philosophical issues. He became legendary for centuries in India for being both a wise philosopher and a fearless conqueror. When Alexander and his army reached the mouth of the Indus in July 325 BC, he turned westward for home.

The confusion following the death of Alexander gave Chandragupta Maurya an opportunity to liberate India from the control of the Greeks. He founded a glorious Mauryan empire in 322 BC. We have learned about many empires that eventually divided and became weak and then they were conquered by another invader. In 268 BC the Mauryan empire had a famous king named Ashoka. After he conquered many cities in India, he saw all of the unhappiness and suffering and destruction that was left behind. He decided to follow the ways of the Buddha and give up violence. He practiced kindness to all. He built hospitals for animals and made laws that would keep people from being cruel to animals.

King Ashoka, decided to erect large pillars in border cities and on trade routes that had inscriptions on them that proclaimed his beliefs. The most well-known of the Ashokan pillars is the one at Sarnath, the site of Buddha's First Sermon where he shared the Four Noble Truths - the dharma or the law. This pillar has a horse on it. It represents the horse that Buddha rode when he left the palace of his family on his journey to discover the meaning of life. Many of the pillars are still in existence

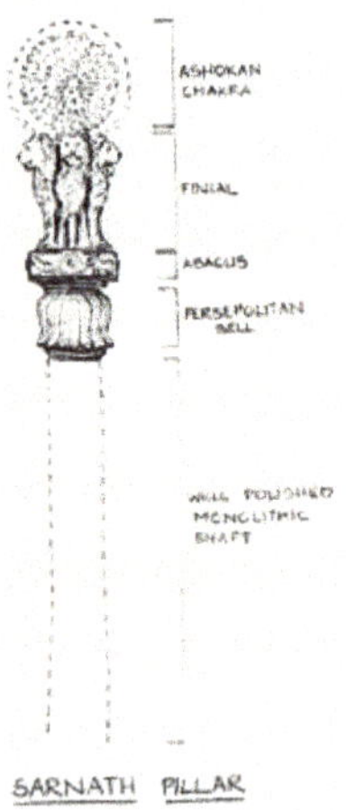

India had a lot to offer to the Romans. Spices like pepper, cloves and cane sugar. The Romans also imported ebony wood and dyes like indigo from India. The Romans were especially interested in the wild animals of India. The Roman coliseum audiences could not get enough of Indian tigers, rhinoceroses, elephants and boas. In exchange, the Roman merchants brought wine, copper, tin, lead and elaborately crafted luxury goods. It was mostly gold and silver coins that went to India, much to the annoyance of the Roman politicians. Remember how they did not like trading with China either?

Roman traders took the long and dangerous route of crossing the Mediterranean to Egypt. Then again, horses played an important part in the journey down to the east African shore and then they sailed to the land of India.

CHAPTER 27 ~ Augustus - The First Roman Emperor

We learned that the first emperor of Rome was Augustus. Augustus reformed the tax system, greatly expanded the Empire and protected and united trade, which brought wealth back to Rome. He also founded enduring organizations such as a fire brigade, a police force and a standing army. Due to Augustus' cultural efforts, Rome became more beautiful, with beautiful temples and other architectural monuments that would impress any visitor. He was also a patron of the arts. He encouraged marriage and childbirth and held a census. According to his census records, the number of Roman citizens grew from four million in 8 BC to five million in 14 AD.

It was during a time of great peace in the reign of Augustus that Jesus Christ was born in Bethlehem. He would have been born in Nazareth, the home of his parents Joseph and Mary, had it not been for the census ordered by Augustus, requiring all adults to register at their ancestral home towns.

Despite all of the good that Augustus accomplished, the Senate, which was meant to represent all of the people, was put on a path toward unimportance. After all, the rule of an emperor is absolute. Overall, Augustus was a good leader but the next few emperors, well not so much. Eventually the title "emperor" went to some people's heads.

In 2009 fragments of a two-thousand-year-old statue of Emperor Augustus on horseback was found in the Aegean Sea. But what happened to the rest of it? We'll find out.

Mary and Joseph were Jewish people. Since Joseph was a descendant of King David, he had to go to Bethlehem in Judea, David's ancient home, for the census that was ordered by Augustus. The journey from Nazareth to Bethlehem was a long one. Samaria was between Nazareth and Bethlehem. Samaritans and Jews did not get along so some people think that Joseph and Mary took the long way around and avoided Samaria all together making the journey even longer. Good thing they had a donkey. A horse would have been too expensive for poor people like Joseph and Mary but I'm glad my relative, the donkey, could help; horses, donkeys and asses all belong to the same family - Equus Caballus. We are so closely related that a donkey can be successfully bred to a horse. A mule is the result of a horse/donkey cross.

Mary and Joseph had their baby in Bethlehem of Judea in the land that was once called Canaan. We learned about Canaan before. They named the baby Jesus.

Did you know that there is a legend that animals who live in a stable are given the gift of speech at midnight on Christmas? It's a gift to thank the animals for sheltering the baby Jesus and his parents. My humans have yet to catch me talking.

Jesus lived quietly in Judea for thirty years then Jesus started to travel through the region teaching people what God wanted them to do. You can read all about the teachings of Jesus in four books of the New Testament of the Bible. These books were written by his disciples Matthew, Mark, Luke and John. Jesus traveled to many cities teaching, healing the sick and performing many miracles. While he was near Jericho one day, Jesus turned to his twelve disciples and said: "We are going up to Jerusalem." As he got close to the village of Beth-phage, near the Mount of Olives, he gave specific instructions to two of his disciples, sending them to fetch a donkey. Jesus rode into Jerusalem on the donkey and the people cheered for him. Again, my friend the donkey! Many people spread their own clothes and palm branches in the way to honor to Jesus. There were many people cheering for him and they were very excited

As Jesus viewed Jerusalem from the back of the donkey, he began to weep and said, "The days are coming upon you when your enemies will raise a palisade against you; they will encircle you and hem you in on all sides. They will smash you to the ground and your children within you, and they will not leave one stone upon another because you did not recognize the time of your visitation."

True to Jesus' words, Jerusalem's destruction happens – we will learn about that later.

Jesus was very popular with the people and the leaders of Judea were worried that Jesus would lead a rebellion against the Romans. The Roman official that was put in charge of Judea by Augustus was also worried that Jesus, along with the Jewish people, would start a rebellion. That would make him very unpopular with Augustus. So, along with some of the Jewish leaders of Judea, the Romans arrested Jesus, tried him for treason and crucified him.

CHAPTER 29 ~ What year is it now in this book?

Throughout this book, so far when I tell you dates, I have been saying BC after the year. Now I am going to change to AD after the year.

WHY?

A Roman monk named Dionysius Exiguus set up the "AD" system in about 500 AD. AD stands for Anno Domini which in Latin means "in the year of the Lord" and it refers to the year when Jesus Christ was born. He worked backward using Biblical texts to estimate when he thought Jesus was born.

Then about 700 AD, Bede the Venerable called the time before AD "ante uero incarnationis dominicae tempus," which is Latin for "the time before the Lord's true incarnation." Our English equivalent to that Latin phrase is "Before Christ." - BC

Some references will say BCE for BC and CE for AD. BCE means before Common Era and CE means Common Era. For some, BCE and CE do not relate to faith in Christ and seem more appropriate. However, the numbers are still exactly the same and still have an end and start at the traditional year of the birth of Jesus Christ.

CHAPTER 30 ~ Some Really Bad Emperors and the Praetorian Guard

Augustus was a good emperor but, with a title like "emperor", chances are there are going to be some that get carried away with power.

Augustus was emperor from 27 BC to 14 AD. The next emperor was Tiberius. He reigned from 14 AD to 37 AD. He became a tyrannical hermit, imposing a reign of terror against many important Romans. The only real threat to his power, the Roman Senate, was afraid of his personal body guards called the Praetorian Guard.

When Tiberius died, Caligula became emperor. His reign of terror only lasted from 37 AD to 41 AD. Caligula was quoted as saying, "Remember that I have the right to do anything to anybody." He made high-ranking senators run for miles in front of his chariot. He drained the treasury with his excesses faster than it could be replenished with taxes. A plan to end his reign of terror was formed between the Praetorian Guard, the Senate and the equestrian order. In late January of 41 AD Caligula was stabbed to death by officers of the Praetorian Guard.

Claudius was the next emperor from 41 AD to 54 AD. In some ways he was a welcome relief. He brought peace to Rome with the restoration of the rule of law. But he was paranoid and worried about being assassinated. His paranoia did not stop with conspirators. He had problems with the Jews in Rome so to avoid further rioting, he had them all expelled from the city. His paranoia was well founded. Claudius was not to die naturally.

Claudius died shortly after eating poisoned mushrooms that were given to him by his beloved wife. She wanted her son Nero to become emperor. Nero soon ascended to the throne of the Empire and a new era of corruption began. Nero ruled Rome from 54 AD until his death by suicide in 68 AD. He is best known for his evil ways, political murders and persecution of Christians.

Sculpture of Nero as part of the Cesares de Roma project

Early in the morning of June 19, 64 AD a blaze broke out in the shops around the Circus Maximus and quickly spread throughout the city. Over the next nine days, three of Rome's fourteen districts were destroyed and an additional seven were severely damaged. Nero used up all of the Roman treasury rebuilding the city around his one hundred acre "Golden House". In addition, revolts in Britain and Judea cost even more money. Rather than stay in Rome to handle the problems, he left for Greece and competed in the Olympic games as a charioteer. When Nero returned to Rome in 68 AD there were more revolts in Gaul, Spain and Africa. Soon the Praetorian Guard, along with the Senate decided to no longer support Nero. They declared Nero an enemy of the people. Nero learned that they planned to arrest him and execute him so, he took his own life instead.

The Praetorian Guard and Equestrian Order seem to be even more powerful than the emperors. Who were they?

The Equites were the second of the property-based classes of ancient Rome, ranking below the senatorial class. A member of the equestrian order was known as an Eques. So, I guess having horses made a person very important!

The Praetorian Guard - an elite unit of soldiers - was one of the most distinctive features of Roman imperial rule. Only the best, most deserving and physically-trained soldiers were accepted into the guard. Half were foot soldiers and half were cavalry. They were equipped with the latest weapons and they underwent extremely difficult training in ancient martial arts.

Their primary role was the personal protection of the Emperor, but they also functioned as a police force both in Rome and other Italian cities.

86

Augustus formed the Praetorian Guard. He recruited fifteen cohorts of about five hundred men each. Each cohort eventually swelled to one thousand men. Three of the nine units were stationed in Rome while the other six were stationed throughout Italy. Each cohort was under the command of an Eques. The elite cavalry arm of the Praetorian Guard formed the personal cavalry bodyguard of the Roman Emperor.

The Praetorian Guard was responsible for the overthrow or murder of fifteen out of the first forty-eight emperors who governed Rome between 27 BC and 305 AD. Constantine saw the danger of trusting the Praetorians any further and disbanded the units that remained, scattering the soldiers all over the empire. We'll learn more about Constantine.

CHAPTER 31 ~ The Destruction of Jerusalem

Do you remember all the things that happened to the Jewish people? The Jewish people were ruled by many other people for a long time. They lived in Egypt for a long time and then the pharaoh made them slaves. Moses moved them to Canaan then the Assyrians captured them and took them to Assyria. Then Babylon captured Assyria and took the Israelites to Babylon. Finally, Cyrus the Great allowed them to return to their home in Canaan. Then along came the Romans who ruled over the Israelites.

Judea was the Roman name for the Land of Israel. This meant not only the area called Judea in Israel - known as the West Bank today - it also included the whole area inhabited by the Jews.

Finally, the Jewish people had enough. They revolted in 66 AD. They forced the Romans out of Jerusalem. Jerusalem was a very important city to the Jewish people. The Temple where they worshiped God was in Jerusalem.

A revolutionary government was then set up by the Israelites. Nero sent the Roman army to crush the rebellion. As we already learned, the Jewish people did not have horses; they did not have a cavalry. Overwhelmed by the Roman army and cavalry, the Jewish forces fled the city. On August 29, in 70 AD Jerusalem fell. The Temple was burned and the Jewish state collapsed. So, true to Jesus' words, Jerusalem's destruction happened. But the Jewish people continued to revolt.

After putting down the third rebellion in 136 AD and enslaving many of the survivors, Emperor Hadrian ordered that all Jews be exiled from the area. He took the name of the ancient enemies of Israel, the Philistines, Latinized it to Palestine, and applied it to the Land of Israel. He hoped to erase the name Israel from all memory. Some Jewish people settled on the border of what was their homeland but many scattered to numerous countries. Isn't it interesting to learn about how places in the world, that we hear so much about today, came to be and why people who live there are still arguing about rights to the land?

CHAPTER 32 ~ Persecution of the Christians and then …
Constantine

The Jewish people were not the only ones persecuted by the Romans. After Jesus Christ died, many people followed his teachings. They were called Christians. The Romans worshiped many gods. Emperors even considered themselves gods and demanded that the people worship them. The Christians would not do that. The Romans worried that this new group of people would become strong and powerful and overthrow Rome so the Christians were persecuted and executed; they were put in jail and forced to fight lions in the Colosseum.

Through the centuries, the Roman emperors continued to persecute the Christians. But Rome had more to fear from itself than from the Christians. A total of twenty-two emperors took the throne in the third century, many of them meeting violent ends from the powerful Praetorian Guard.

The reign of Diocletian 284 AD to 305 AD restored peace and wealth in Rome. Diocletian divided the empire. Diocletian and Galerius ruled the eastern Roman Empire, while Maximian and Constantius took power in the west.

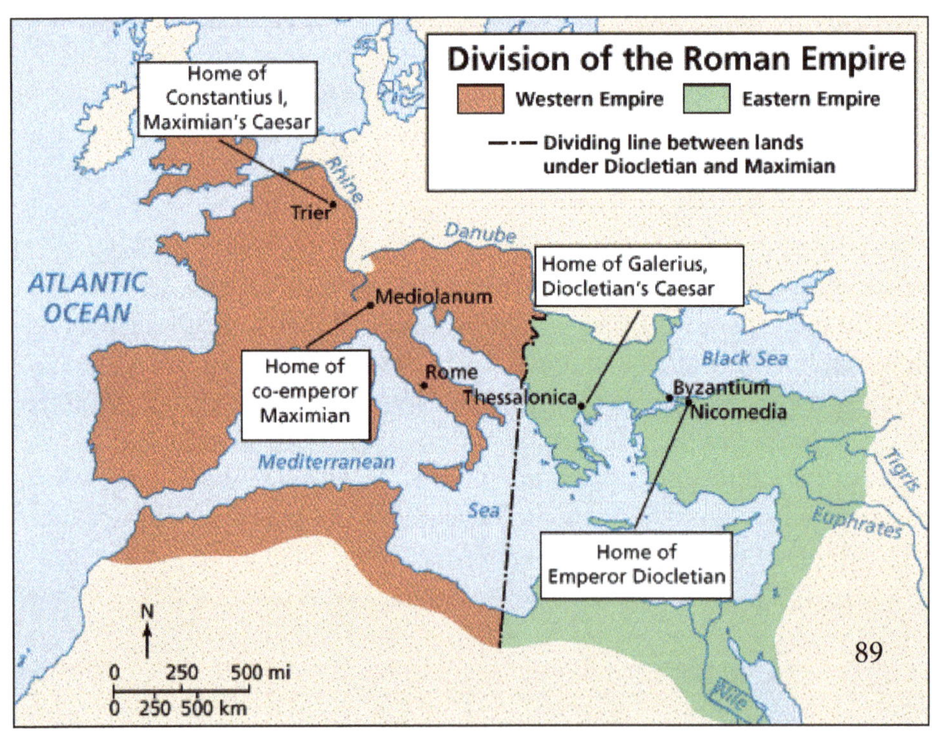

After Diocletian and Maximian retired from office the entire system fell apart. There was a power struggle – again! In the spring of 311 AD, with forty thousand soldiers behind him, Constantine (the son of Constantius) rode toward Rome to confront an enemy whose numbers were four times his own. Maxentius, vying for supremacy in the West, waited in Rome with his Italian troops and the elite Praetorian Guard, confident no one could successfully invade the city. But Constantine's army was already overwhelming his foes in Italy as he marched toward the capital. Maxentius turned to pagan oracles, finding a prophecy that the "enemy of the Romans" would perish. But Constantine was still miles away. So, believing the prophecy, Maxentius boldly and confidently marched out of the city to meet his foe. If he had stayed in the city his chances of winning the battle would have been better – but he believed the prophecy.

Constantine saw a vision too. It was a bright cross with the words "by this sign conquer." Constantine believed that Christ himself told him in a dream to take the cross into battle as his standard. When he awoke early the next morning, he ordered his soldiers to mark their shields with the Chi-Rho.

Maxentius gathered his army on the bank of the Tiber. He had cut the bridge itself, but in case of defeat he could retreat to Rome across a temporary bridge made of boats.

Constantine personally led his cavalry against that of the enemy. Riding at the front, his gold-gilded armor sparkled in the sun's rays. From walk to trot, Constantine's barbarian horsemen accelerated to a gallop and sliced through the enemy ranks. The Numidian and Moorish light cavalry of Maxentius were no match for Constantine's Celts and Germans or for Constantine himself. His spear struck down many foes, to be unhorsed and trampled beneath his horse's hooves. Horses, along with Constantine's leadership, were again the key element of the victory. Maxentius' men were driven in flight across the bridge of boats, which collapsed under them. Maxentius attempted to escape over the bridge of boats too but his own army-turned-mob, pressing through the narrow passage, forced him into the river, where he drowned by the weight of his armor. Alone among Maxentius' soldiers, the Praetorian Guard valiantly stood their ground. It was the last battle in their three-hundred-year history and they went out in a blaze of glory. This battle was called the Battle of the Milvian Bridge

Constantine entered Rome as the undisputed ruler of the West. He was the first Roman emperor with a cross on the shields of his army and cavalry. He moved the Roman capital to the Greek city of Byzantium, which he renamed Constantinople. At the Council of Nicaea in 325 AD Constantine made Christianity Rome's official religion. His conversion to Christianity had far reaching effects on the practice of Christianity.

The Arch of Constantine is a triumphal arch in Rome. It is located between the Colosseum and the Palatine Hill. It was erected by the Roman Senate to commemorate Constantine's victory over Maxentius at the Battle of Milvian Bridge. A picture on the arch depicts the battle.

Roman security and prosperity under Constantine were temporary. Thirty years after his death, the Western Roman Empire had many internal conflicts and was threatened by outside invaders that the Romans called barbarians. Fighting off the barbarians became costly and the Western Roman Empire grew poor. The first of these invaders were the Goths.

In 402 AD the Romans moved their capital from Rome to Ravenna in northeastern Italy because it was, supposedly, easier to defend. In the same year Alaric, the king of the Visigoths invaded Italy but was turned back. Another Gothic warlord, Radagaisus, tried again in 406 AD but was stopped. The Visigoths kept coming! In 410 AD Alaric was back in Italy attacking Rome. This time, on the night of August 24, 410 AD rebel slaves quietly opened the gates of Rome to admit the Visigoths. The Visigoths embarked on a three-day spree of plunder and destruction that left Rome a smoking ruin.

Who were the Goths? The Goths were a Germanic tribe. Visigoths were western Goths and Ostrogoths were eastern Goths.

The Goth's reputation as barbarians comes from the Romans who viewed them as second-class subjects of the Empire. However, the Goths were largely peaceful hunters and farmers. They were skilled in horsemanship and archery; the Goths army was mostly made up of cavalry. They were fierce fighters. Their cavalry engaged in close combat backed up by archers on horseback. Since for the most part, they were no match for the Roman Empire, they relied on surprise, treachery or siege warfare. The job of the Roman cavalry was mainly to protect the flanks and pursue fleeing enemies. The Goths on the other hand used the cavalry to attack. Horses – a decisive factor – AGAIN!

The Vandals were also a barbarian Germanic tribe. They were able to take advantage of Roman weakness in the provinces of the Western Roman Empire and on December 31, 406 AD a group of Vandals crossed the Rhine River and advanced into Gaul. At first, the Vandal march into Roman territory did not attract much attention from the Roman Empire. Since they were ignored by the Roman Empire, the Vandals made their way to Iberia which is modern-day Spain and Portugal. In 422 AD the Vandals won a battle against the Romans in a port city of Spain which then allowed the Vandals to invade Africa. In 435 AD the Romans made a peace treaty in which much of North Africa was given to the Vandals. In 439 AD the Vandals broke the treaty, captured the city of Carthage and moved their capital there. The Vandals advanced into Sicily. With the Vandals now in control of Rome's grain supply, the Western Roman Empire was in big trouble! In 455 the Vandals invaded Rome.

Guess what? The Vandals had amazing horsemanship skills too. An important role for a Vandal was raising horses for warfare. Roman officers said that the horses of the Vandals were not remarkable for beauty or speed and they were not trained to do maneuvers as the Roman horses were. But the Vandal's method of fighting with cavalry was different; they would ride straight ahead and did not fear hand to hand combat. How fearsome that must have been! They were perhaps unsophisticated compared to the Romans but they relied on shock and that seemed to work for them. Horses – a decisive factor – AGAIN!

Do you remember the story I told you about the fragments of a two-thousand-year-old statue of Emperor Augustus on horseback that was found in the Aegean Sea? Now it's time to find out what happened to the rest of it.

The statue was originally located in a town more than one hundred miles deep inside Germanic territory. In 9 AD Germanic forces defeated three Roman legions. The crushing defeat left Roman cities to the west in Gaul totally undefended. Augustus dropped his plans for colonizing Germany - forever changing the course of European history. The Romans would have removed the splendid statue and transported it back across the Rhine, had they been able to do so. The shattered remnants are seen as proof of sudden chaos after the military disaster.

Archaeologists believe that triumphant Germanic warriors captured the town and pulled down the statue. The gilded-bronze horse head was found at the bottom of the town's central well. In keeping with Germanic religious rites, the horse's head was ritually "drowned" in the well so as to appease the cult of the horse. The rest of the statue was smashed to bits.

Can you see now the beginnings of how the Germanic tribes became powerful?

In 370 AD the Huns crossed the Volga River and conquered the Alans, another civilization of nomadic, warring horsemen. Two years later, they attacked the Ostrogoths. By 376, the Huns had attacked the Visigoths. Some of the Alans, Goths and Visigoths were drafted into the army of the Huns. The Huns earned a reputation as ruthless and unstoppable. In 395 AD they began invading Roman lands. In 434 Attila became king of the Huns.

Who were the Huns?

The Huns spent one full century inflicting havoc and destruction. We have talked about the horsemanship skills of Romans, Persians, Assyrians, Egyptians and many others. The conqueror always had better horsemanship skills than the defeated and thus became the conquerors. But the skill of the Huns with horses was superior to anything ever seen before! Their horsemanship is what made the Huns so fearsome and unbeatable.

Following a nomadic lifestyle, the Huns seemed to the Romans as if they were glued to their saddles. Some historians mention them as doing almost everything from atop their horses: even eating and sleeping. The Huns were taught to ride a horse as early as they could walk, at which time they were also taught how to fire a bow from atop their horse. The Hunnic bow was an engineering marvel of the time. It was a reflex bow, which means that when strung, it bent back upon itself, giving it more tension than any other bow of its time. A warrior could inflict a deadly shot at eighty yards and fire an arrow three times that distance. Unlike the other saddles used by the Romans and other Europeans, the Hun saddles had a high front and rear section. This helped the rider to be very steady in the saddle; almost as if he was fixed to his horse. This way he could twist and turn in a three hundred sixty-degree angle without the risk of falling off, all while firing his long-range bow in all directions.

The Huns also usually made use of the lasso in battle. They would usually fight and travel in relatively small numbers, no more than a few hundred riders. If they encountered an enemy, they would dash in and strike with lightning speed and then retreat, only to reappear elsewhere and strike again.

The Romans recognized the benefits of having the Huns on their side. Instead of fighting each other, the Romans employed the Huns to fight for them as mercenaries. The Romans promised the Huns great riches if they would fight for them. The Romans had great riches so this was an offer Atilla, the leader of the Huns, could not refuse. Originally the Romans paid the Huns as mercenaries but eventually, they found they were paying the Huns not to invade the Roman Empire rather than help the Roman empire attack others..

Attila was a brutal leader leaving a path of destruction and slaughter wherever he went. The Huns relied heavily on loot and plunder to survive. Attila knew that in order to guarantee the continued loyalty of his men, he would need to supply them with a constant supply of gold. To do so, he would have to set his sights on much bigger prizes than ever before, focusing his attention now on the Roman Empire itself.

Constantinople in the Eastern Roman Empire was his first target. The city had very good defense systems and could easily have defeated Atilla. Some of Atilla's own men knew that Atilla could not defeat the city so they deserted and took refuge inside the city. But Atilla's reputation was so frightening that Constantinople paid off the Huns with six thousand pounds of gold to make them go away. Attila demanded the deserters be returned to him. As punishment for their lack of loyalty, Attila had them all impaled, leaving them to suffer a horrible death, suspended on spikes for up to two days before they finally perished.

Now Attila headed for the Western Roman Empire.

The Romans joined forces with their former rivals, the Visigoths, as well as the Alans and they were victorious over the Huns. This victory for the Romans guaranteed that the Western Europe would be spared from the savage Huns.

One year later, in 452 AD Attila was out for revenge. His target was the Italian Peninsula. He and his men crossed the Alps and began ransacking northwestern Italy. Amazingly though, the Huns decided to turn back home. Some people believe that they just wanted to go home and some believe there was a plague killing off his army. Whatever the case, Attila would die of a severe nose bleed one year later and his mighty and terrible kingdom would collapse due to the many internal struggles for power. With his death, the Huns disappeared from Europe as swiftly as they appeared, one hundred years prior.

CHAPTER 35 ~ The Fall of the Roman Empire

The attacks on Rome were not over with the departure of the Huns.

Odoacer was a German warrior. In about 470 AD he entered Italy and joined the Roman army and rose to a position of command.

At the time, the emperor and generals were squabbling among themselves – as usual! The emperor Julius Nepos was overthrown by the Roman general Orestes in 475 AD.

Romulus Augustus was the son of Orestes. He was just a child at the time but Orestes made him the emperor and for about twelve months, Orestes ruled Italy in his son's name.

Orestes promised to give land to tribal leaders in Italy but then backed out of the deal. Odoacer led his tribesmen in a revolt against Orestes. Odoacer's forces captured and executed Orestes on August 28, 476 AD. Romulus was spared because he was only a child.

Odoacer's troops proclaimed him king of Italy, bringing an end to the long history of ancient Rome. Why did Odoacer choose not to be the next emperor of the Roman Empire? The Roman people were still around and the Senate still existed. In fact, he had the backing of the Senate to rule Italy. The basic problem is that to be a Roman emperor, you had to be Roman. Odoacer wasn't.

The Roman empire in western Europe, which had been in existence for five hundred years, ceased to exist. A single emperor was replaced with many kings and princes. Many of these rulers, like Odoacer himself, were non-Roman. Their power was based on the control of military forces made up of Anglo-Saxons in Britain, Goths in southern Gaul and Spain and Vandals in North Africa.

The Eastern Roman Empire–later known as the Byzantine Empire–would remain largely in existence for centuries to come.

Few people in most of the Western Roman Empire knew about Odoacer or even cared who was in charge. Remember, they did not have social media to spread the news and have all sorts of opinions and ideas about what might happen next. After all, by now most of the provinces that once made up the Western Roman Empire were under the control of various "barbarian" powers. Gaul was divided into areas controlled by Franks, Burgundians and Visigoths. Spain was divided between Visigoths and a German tribe called Suevi. North Africa was now a Vandal Kingdom.

Of the former provinces of the Western Empire only Britain fought on, resisting Germanic occupation. We'll learn more about the Britains in another book all about knights and Medieval times.

In this book you learned how very important horses have been to the history of the world so far. Just wait until you find out what happens next! My stablemate, Tyson, will take you on a journey through the Middles Ages and meet the knights and horses of Medieval times in the next book, "Dark to Light".

SOURCES

Dear Reader,

Many sources were used to gather the information for this book. Those sources are listed here along with many other additional sources. If you would like to learn more about any of the topics in this book, you may want to refer to some of these sources. Did the games in the Colosseum and Circus Maximus sound exciting? Maybe Hannibal crossing the Alps with horses and elephants was something you want to know more about. I hope you had fun learning about all of these things and that your imagination is just spinning and that you can't wait to learn more!

Hark

CHAPTER 2
http://www.annarbor.com/pets/the-evolution-of-the-modern-equine-was-impacted-by-grass-and-humans/
https://www.khanacademy.org/partner-content/big-history-project/early-humans/how-did-first-humans-live/a/gallery-how-did-the-first-humans-live
https://www.wired.com/2011/11/cave-painting-colors/
https://www.khanacademy.org/partner-content/big-history-project/expansion-interconnection/other-materials8/a/a-little-big-history-of-horses
https://www.archaeology.org/issues/180-1507/features/3349-warhorses

CHAPTER 3
https://www.ancient.eu/chariot/
http://www.armeniapast.com/forgotten-kingdom-revised/

CHAPTER 4
https://www.bobspixels.com/kaibab.org/geology/gc065mya.htm
https://www.livescience.com/4180-sahara-desert-lush-populated.html

CHAPTER 6
http://www.learnmartialartsinchina.com/kung-fu-school-blog/why-is-china-called-the-middle-kingdom/
https://antiquities.co.uk/Collections/the-horse-in-chinese-art-and-culture.html
http://www.edubilla.com/invention/saddle/
http://www.limebrook.com/saddlehistory.html
http://factsanddetails.com/china/cat2/sub1/item42.html
https://www.jstor.org/stable/4629341?seq=1#page_scan_tab_contents (did not read /use yet)

https://china.usc.edu/sites/default/files/forums/Chinese%20Inventions.pdf
https://www.ncbi.nlm.nih.gov/pmc/articles/PMC2287209/
https://en.wikipedia.org/wiki/Dynasties_in_Chinese_history
https://en.wikipedia.org/wiki/Horses_in_East_Asian_warfare
http://dsr.nii.ac.jp/rarebook/02/index.html.en
http://www.icm.gov.mo/rc/viewer/20009/883 excellent
https://www.travelchinaguide.com/china_great_wall/history/

CHAPTER 7
http://www.npl.co.uk/educate-explore/factsheets/history-of-length-measurement/
https://www.history.com/topics/ancient-history/nefertiti
https://www.khanacademy.org/humanities/ancient-art-civilizations/egypt-art/
new-kingdom/a/paintings-from-the-tomb-chapel-of-nebamun
http://horsehints.org/Breeds/NiseanExtinct.htm
https://alchetron.com/Nisean-horse

CHAPTER 8
https://www.ancient.eu/Hyksos/
https://www.archaeology.org/issues/309-1809/features/6855-egypt-hyksos-for-
eign-dynasty

CHAPTER 9
https://www.biblicalarchaeology.org/daily/a-history-of-horses-in-the-divided-
kingdom-of-israel-and-judah/
http://www.ganttstreetbaptist.org/article.aspx?auid=1426
https://www.heraldofhope.org.au/horses-chariots/
https://www.bibletools.org/index.cfm/fuseaction/Topical.show/RTD/CGG/
ID/13349/Multiplying-Horses.htm
http://www.womeninthebible.net/war-in-the-bible/horses-chariot/

CHAPTER 10
https://www.enotes.com/homework-help/why-were-assyrians-strong-199003
https://www.ancient.eu/nineveh/
https://www.ancient.eu/Hanging_Gardens_of_Babylon/

CHAPTER 11
https://www.livescience.com/4846-eruption-thera-changed-world.html
https://www.nationalgeographic.com/archaeology-and-history/maga-
zine/2017/09-10/Minoan_Crete/
http://www.salimbeti.com/micenei/chariots.htm
https://www.ancient.eu/Greek_Dark_Age/

CHAPTER 12
https://www.history.com/topics/ancient-history/trojan-war
CHAPTER 13
https://www.olympic.org/ancient-olympic-games/chariot-racing
https://www.amnh.org/exhibitions/horse/how-we-shaped-horses-how-horses-shaped-us/sport/the-chariot-race
http://ancientolympics.arts.kuleuven.be/eng/TC008aEN.html
https://www.topendsports.com/sport/extinct/chariot-racing.htm

CHAPTER 14
The Story of the World
https://sites.google.com/site/historyofthewarhorse1/horses-in-the-ancient-world/persia-arabia
https://www.ancient.eu/Darius_I/
CHAPTER 15
https://www.britannica.com/biography/Xenophon
https://thegreatthinkers.org/xenophon/biography/
http://imh.org/exhibits/online/legacy-of-the-horse/xenophon-father-classical-equitation/index.html
https://www.historyoftheancientworld.com/2011/06/did-alexander-the-great-read-xenophon/
https://sites.google.com/site/historyofthewarhorse1/horses-in-the-ancient-world/greece

CHAPTER 16
https://theworldofalexanderthegreat.wordpress.com/tag/xenophon/
https://www.awesomestories.com/asset/view/ASSASSINATION-OF-PHILIP-II-Alexander-the-Great
https://www.history.com/topics/ancient-history/alexander-the-great
https://www.sparknotes.com/biography/alexander/summary/
https://www.mnn.com/earth-matters/animals/photos/10-famous-horses-from-history/Bucephalus

CHAPTER 18
https://www.ducksters.com/history/ancient_rome/republic_to_empire.php
https://www.historycrunch.com/republic-vs-empire-in-ancient-rome.html#/
http://www.zocalopublicsquare.org/2018/02/16/many-statues-men-horseback/ideas/essay/

CHAPTER 19 and 20
https://www.historycrunch.com/republic-vs-empire-in-ancient-rome.html#/
https://www.nationalgeographic.org/news/romes-transition-republic-empire/
http://www.livius.org/articles/person/caesar/caesar-04/
https://www.warhistoryonline.com/guest-bloggers/caesars-elite-germanic-caval-ry.html/2
https://ludwigheinrichdyck.wordpress.com/2016/05/30/caesars-elite-german-ic-cavalry/
https://www.history.com/topics/ancient-history/ancient-rome
https://www.ancient.eu/article/910/the-sack-of-rome-by-the-gauls-390-bce/
https://www.worldhistory.biz/prehistory/89895-the-celtic-cavalry.html
https://warfarehistorynetwork.com/daily/military-history/the-war-chariots-of-the-celtic-elite/
https://www.history.com/topics/ancient-history/hannibal
https://www.heritage-history.com/index.php?c=resources&s=war-dir&f=wars_ro-manmacedon
https://www.honga.net/totalwar/rome2/unit.php?l=en&v=rome2&f=gaul_arv-erni&u=Cel_Noble_Horse
https://celticgaulsdotcom.wordpress.com/gaul-culture/

CHAPTER 21
http://imh.org/exhibits/online/legacy-of-the-horse/roman-roads/index.html
https://www.britannica.com/topic/Appian-Way
https://www.history.com/news/8-ways-roads-helped-rome-rule-the-ancient-world
https://www.ancient.eu/Silk_Road/
https://sublimechina.com/silk-road-facts-interesting-internet/
https://www.telegraph.co.uk/news/world/china-watch/culture/tianma-chi-nas-heavenly-horses/
https://www.mircorp.com/horses-silk-road/
https://www.topchinatravel.com/silk-road/animals-in-silk-road.htm
http://theconversation.com/silk-road-trading-helped-produce-the-modern-horse-17856
http://www.wagmag.com/on-the-old-silk-road-with-chinas-celestial-horses/
https://sinosphere.blogs.nytimes.com/2014/05/13/the-horse-at-the-heart-of-chi-nese-turkmen-relations/
https://www.revolvy.com/page/War-of-the-Heavenly-Horses
https://blogs.wsj.com/chinarealtime/2014/05/13/chinas-president-gets-a-heaven-ly-new-pony/
http://www.hitsshows.com/hits-blog/3-horses-that-changed-history

CHAPTER 22
https://interestingengineering.com/the-rise-and-fall-of-roman-aqueducts
https://www.advantour.com/uzbekistan/legends/heavenly-horses.htm
https://www.english-heritage.org.uk/visit/places/chesters-roman-fort-and-museum-hadrians-wall/history/absence-of-stables/

CHAPTER 23
https://www.npr.org/templates/story/story.php?storyId=130190252
https://www.history.com/topics/ancient-history/mark-antony

CHAPTER 24
https://www.ancient.eu/article/637/roman-daily-life/
https://www.ducksters.com/history/ancient_rome/life_in_the_country.php
https://www.ancient.eu/article/638/trade-in-the-roman-world/
https://www.thevintagenews.com/2018/03/01/colosseum-naval-battles/
https://www.ancient.eu/Circus_Maximus/
https://earlychurchhistory.org/entertainment/famous-horses-in-romes-chariot-races/
https://www.historyanswers.co.uk/ancient/death-glory-and-chariot-racing/
https://eaglesanddragonspublishing.com/chariot-racing-in-ancient-rome/
https://chestofbooks.com/animals/horses/Health-Disease-Treatment-4/The-Horses-Of-Rome.html

CHAPTER 25
https://www.ancient.eu/article/208/cultural-links-between-india--the-greco-roman-worl/
http://knowindia.gov.in/culture-and-heritage/ancient-history/alexander.php
https://www.awesomestories.com/asset/view/ELEPHANTS-IN-WAR-Alexander-the-Great

CHAPTER 26
https://www.coinsweekly.com/en/Archive/Globalisation-in-Roman-times-Trade-with-India/8?&id=698&type=a
https://economictimes.indiatimes.com/blogs/SilkStalkings/trade-links-with-rome-go-back-2000-years/

CHAPTER 27
https://www.historyhit.com/democracy-vs-grandeur-was-augustus-good-or-bad-for-rome/
CHAPTER 28
https://christianity.stackexchange.com/questions/16081/from-where-does-the-tradition-come-that-mary-rode-on-a-donkey-to-bethlehem-prior

CHAPTER 29
https://www.quora.com/Who-invented-the-present-calendar-How-did-they-know-BC-and-AD
https://englandsnortheast.co.uk/jarrow-bede/

CHAPTER 30
https://www.ancient.eu/claudius/
https://www.history.com/topics/ancient-history/caligula
http://www.ancientpages.com/2018/05/26/praetorian-guard-roman-elite-unit-assigned-to-protect-but-also-involved-in-confinement-execution-spying-and-threats/
https://www.unrv.com/military/praetorian-guard.php
https://www.realmofhistory.com/2017/09/19/14-praetorian-guard-facts/
https://www.boredpanda.com/ancient-sculptures-of-roman-emperors-cesares-de-roma/

CHAPTER 31
https://www.britannica.com/event/First-Jewish-Revolt
https://focusonjerusalem.com/whatromecalledthepromisedland.html
http://www.religioustolerance.org/name_mide.htm

CHAPTER 32
https://www.christianitytoday.com/history/people/rulers/constantine.html
https://www.historytoday.com/richard-cavendish/battle-milvian-bridge
https://warfarehistorynetwork.com/daily/military-history/emperor-constantine-the-great/
https://www.teggelaar.com/en/rome-day-3-continuation-7/

CHAPTER 33
https://www.historytoday.com/richard-cavendish/visigoths-sack-rome
https://www.ancient.eu/Goths/
https://en.wikipedia.org/wiki/Gothic_and_Vandal_warfare
http://mentalfloss.com/article/80335/11-rome-sacking-facts-about-original-goths
https://www.history.com/news/who-were-the-goths-and-vandals
https://www.livescience.com/46150-vandals.html
https://www.ancient.eu/Vandals/
Conquerors of the Roam Empire: The Vandals; by Simon MacDowall
http://antinousgaygod.blogspot.com/2015/07/gilded-bronze-equestrian-statue-adorned.html

CHAPER 34
https://www.realmofhistory.com/2015/09/05/8-incredible-facts-about-the-huns-you-probably-didnt-know-about/
https://www.history.com/news/7-legendary-barbarian-weapons

https://www.history.com/topics/ancient-china/huns
https://www.toptenz.net/10-disturbing-facts-attila-huns.php
https://www.ancient.eu/Attila_the_Hun/
https://archeryhistorian.com/hun-bow/

CHAPTER 35
https://www.britannica.com/biography/Odoacer
https://www.britannica.com/biography/Romulus-Augustulus
http://www.bbc.co.uk/history/ancient/romans/fallofrome_article_01.shtml

You may enjoy "The Story of the World" series by Susan Wise Bauer. Much of the time line in "Hoofbeats Through History – No Man to Romans" was inspired by this series. The Series comes with activity books and tests as well.

INDEX

Abraham, 30

Achaean League, 59

Achilles, 38

Aqueducts, 35, 67

Africa, 14, 57, 58, 68, 70, 80, 86, 94, 99

Agamemnon, 38

Ahmose, 28

Ajax, 38

Akhal-Teke, 63

Akhenaten, 23

Alans, 96, 98

Alaric, 93

Alexander the Great, 47, 48, 50, 77

America, 12-13

Appian Way, 64

Archaeologist, 4, 5, 7, 16, 24, 29, 95

Armenia(n), 6, 7, 11, 43

Ashoka, 79

Ashurnasirpal, 34,35

Assyrians, 18, 34, 35, 42, 52, 88, 96

Athens, 34, 44, 46, 47

Atilla, 97-98

Augustus, 68, 81, 82, 83, 85, 87, 94, 95, 99

Babylon, 11, 35, 42, 49, 52, 88

Barbarians, 19, 20, 37, 56, 93

Bethlehem, 81, 82

Brutus, 68

Bucephalus, 47, 48, 50

Buddha, 78, 79

Byzantine Empire, 100

Caligula, 76, 85

Canaan, 30, 32, 43, 42, 82, 88

Carthage, 32, 57, 58, 94

Caspian horse, 43

Cassius, 68

Castes, 78

Cavalry, 33, 43, 44, 46, 47, 48, 49, 56, 57, 59, 62, 78, 86, 87, 88, 91, 92, 93, 94

Celts, 56, 91

Chariots, 6-10, 11, 14, 15, 27, 28, 29, 31, 33, 35, 37, 40, 41, 42, 52, 71, 73, 74, 75

China, 10, 11, 15-21, 52, 61, 62, 63, 64, 65, 80

Chi-Rho, 90

Chauvet Cave, 4

Christians, 53, 85, 89

Circus Maximus, 10, 71, 73, 75, 86

Claudius, 85

Cleopatra, 68

Colosseum, 71, 73, 89, 92

Constantine, 53, 87, 89, 90, 91, 92, 93

Constantinople, 26,92, 98

Constantius, 89, 90

Crete, 36

Cyrus, 42, 43, 44, 46, 77, 88

Darius, 45, 49

Dark Ages of Greece, 37

Dayuan 62, 63

Diocletian, 89, 90

Donkey, 63, 64, 70, 82, 83

Eastern Roman Empire 89, 98, 100

Eastern Zhou Dynasty, 20

Egypt, Egyptians, 8,11,14,16,23,27-33,49, 52, 68, 70,77, 80, 88, 96

Eighteenth Dynasty, 28

Equestrian Order, 85, 86

Equi magni, 33

Equus, 1, 82

Exodus, 32, 33

Farming, Farmes, Farmer 16,70, 74, 77, 93

Ferghana Valley, 62

Galerius, 89

Gaul, 56, 59, 60, 70, 86, 95, 99, 100

Germanic tribes, 95

Gladiator, 71

Gods, 30,44, 89

Great Wall, 20,21

Greece, Greeks, 26, 36, 37, 38, 39, 40, 43, 44, 45, 46, 47, 48, 49, 52, 55, 58, 70, 77, 79, 86, 92

Han Dynasty, 18

Hannibal, 57, 58

Hands (horse measurement), 22,43, 62

Harness, 15,16, 41,52

Heavenly Horses, 62, 63

Helen, 38

Hinduism, 77

Hittite, 8,23,25

Homer, 38

Huns, 96-99

Hyksos, 27-29,31

Illiad, 38

Incitatus, 76

India, 11, 42, 49, 52, 64, 77-79, 80

Isaac, 30

Israel, Israelites, 30-33,34,52, 88

Jacob, 30

Jerusalem, 82, 83, 88

Jesus, 81, 82-83, 84, 88, 89

Jews, Jewish, 42, 70, 82, 85, 88, 89

Joseph, 30

Joseph (and Mary,) 81, 82

Judea,82, 83, 86, 88

Julius Caesar, 58, 59-60, 68

Kikkuli, 6, 8, 9, 10, 25

Kimon, 40, 41

Lasso, 7

Macedonia, 48, 50, 58

Marc Antony, 60, 68

Mauryan Empire, 79

Maximian, 89, 90

Maxentius, 90, 91, 92

Median horses, 43

Mesopotamia, 8, 16, 34, 77

Middle Kingdom, 15,20

Milvian Bridge, 91, 92

Minoans, 36

Mitanni, 6,8,9

Moses 31,88

Mycenaeans, 36-37

Nebamun, 25

Nefertiti, 23,24
Nero,85, 86, 88
Nestor, 38
Nineveh, 35
Nisean Horse, 26, 43
Nomads, 3, 5, 6, 10, 19, 20, 52
Numidian, 74, 91
Octavian, 68
Odoacer, 99, 100
Odysseus, 38
Odyssey, 38
Olympic Games, 10,40, 86
Orestes, 99
Paris, 38
Paleontologist, 12
Palestine, 88
Patrician, 55
Pax Romana, 69
Persians, 40, 42, 43, 45, 46, 52, 96
Petroglyph, 6
Pharaohs, 10, 23, 28, 30, 31, 33, 88
Philip, 48, 50, 58
Philistines, 88
Phoenicians, 32
Pliny the Elder, 64
Pompey, 60
Porus, 79
Praetorian Guard, 85-87, 89, 90, 91
Punic Wars, 57-58
Ramesses II, 28
Qin Shi Huang, Emperor, 20
Red Sea, 31
Reflex bow, 96
Rice, 16
Roman Republic, 55-58, 59, 68
Romulus Augustus, 99
Saddle, 17, 18, 44, 65, 96
Sahara Desert, 14
Scorpus, 73
Scythian horses, 43

Senate, Roman, 55, 60, 68, 81, 85, 96, 92, 99
Shang Dynasty, 15, 16
Shennong, 18
Siddhartha, 78
Silk, Silk Road, 19, 61, 62, 63, 64, 65
Sparta, 38, 40, 44, 46
Steppe, 19, 20, 21, 77
Stirrup, 15, 17, 44
Tiberius, 85
Trojan War 38
Thirteenth Dynasty, 27
Tutankhamun, 28
Twelfth Dynasty, 27
Twelve Tables, 55
Vandals 93-95, 99
Vedic, 77
Visigoths 93, 96, 98, 100
Western Roman Empire 93, 94, 98, 100
Western Zhou Dynasty, 15, 20
Wu Di, 62, 63
Xenophon, 43, 44, 46-47, 67
Zhang Qian, 62